# Duncan Hines

## Cake Mix Magic

BARNES
& NOBLE
BOOKS

NEW YORK

This edition published by Barnes & Noble, Inc., by arrangement with Publications International, Ltd.

2005 Barnes & Noble Books

**Microwave Cooking:** Microwave ovens vary in wattage. Use the cooking times as guidelines and check for doneness before adding more time.

**Preparation/Cooking Times:** Preparation times are based on the approximate amount of time required to assemble the recipe before cooking, baking, chilling or serving. These times include preparation steps such as measuring, chopping and mixing. The fact that some preparations and cooking can be done simultaneously is taken into account. Preparation of optional ingredients and serving suggestions is not included.

**Pictured on the front cover** *(clockwise from top left):* Boston Cream Pie *(page 128),* Lemon Bars *(page 32),* Chocolate Peanut Butter Cups *(page 144)* and Angel Almond Cupcakes *(page 132).*

**Pictured on the back cover:** Fudge Cake with Melba Topping *(page 148).*

Manufactured in China.

# Contents

42

104

72

# Delicious Cookies

## Orange Pecan Gems

1 package DUNCAN HINES® Moist Deluxe® Orange Supreme Cake Mix
1 container (8 ounces) vanilla low-fat yogurt
1 egg
2 tablespoons butter or margarine, softened
1 cup finely chopped pecans
1 cup pecan halves

**1.** Preheat oven to 350°F. Grease baking sheets.

**2.** Combine cake mix, yogurt, egg, butter and chopped pecans in large bowl. Beat at low speed with electric mixer until well blended. Drop by rounded teaspoonfuls 2 inches apart onto prepared baking sheets. Press pecan half onto center of each cookie. Bake at 350°F for 11 to 13 minutes or until golden brown. Cool 1 minute on baking sheets. Remove to cooling racks. Cool completely. Store in airtight container.     *Makes 4½ to 5 dozen cookies*

5

## Chocolate Almond Biscotti

**1 package DUNCAN HINES® Moist Deluxe® Dark Chocolate Cake Mix**
**1 cup all-purpose flour**
**½ cup butter or margarine, melted**
**2 eggs**
**1 teaspoon almond extract**
**½ cup chopped almonds**
**White chocolate, melted (optional)**

**1.** Preheat oven to 350°F. Line 2 baking sheets with parchment paper.

**2.** Combine cake mix, flour, butter, eggs and almond extract in large bowl. Beat at low speed with electric mixer until well blended; stir in almonds. Divide dough in half. Shape each half into 12×2-inch log; place logs on prepared baking sheets. (Bake logs separately.)

**3.** Bake at 350°F for 30 to 35 minutes or until toothpick inserted in center comes out clean. Remove logs from oven; cool on baking sheets 15 minutes. Using serrated knife, cut logs into ½-inch slices. Arrange slices on baking sheets. Bake biscotti 10 minutes. Remove to cooling racks; cool completely.

**4.** Dip one end of each biscotti in melted white chocolate, if desired. Allow white chocolate to set at room temperature before storing biscotti in airtight container.

*Makes about 2½ dozen cookies*

### Tip

Parchment is heavy paper that is impervious to grease and moisture. It allows for easy removal of cookies from the baking sheets. Parchment paper is sold in sheets and in rolls and is available at gourmet kitchenware stores and at many supermarkets.

## Coconut Clouds

2²⁄₃ cups flaked coconut, divided
1 package DUNCAN HINES® Moist Deluxe® Classic Yellow Cake Mix
1 egg
½ cup vegetable oil
¼ cup water
1 teaspoon almond extract

**1.** Preheat oven to 350°F. Reserve 1¹⁄₃ cups coconut in medium bowl; set aside.

**2.** Combine cake mix, egg, oil, water and almond extract in large bowl. Beat at low speed with electric mixer. Stir in remaining 1¹⁄₃ cups coconut. Drop rounded teaspoonful dough into reserved coconut. Roll to cover lightly. Place on ungreased baking sheet. Repeat with remaining dough, placing balls 2 inches apart. Bake at 350°F for 10 to 12 minutes or until light golden brown. Cool 1 minute on baking sheets. Remove to cooling racks. Cool completely. Store in airtight container.

*Makes 3½ dozen cookies*

**Hint:** To save time when forming dough into balls, use a 1-inch spring-operated cookie scoop. Spring-operated cookie scoops are available at kitchen specialty shops.

## Festive Chocolate Chip Cookies

1 package DUNCAN HINES® Moist Deluxe® Classic White Cake Mix
¼ cup firmly packed light brown sugar
1 egg
¾ cup vegetable oil
1 package (6 ounces) semisweet chocolate chips
½ cup chopped pecans or walnuts
Assorted decors

**1.** Preheat oven to 350°F.

**2.** Combine cake mix, brown sugar, egg and oil in large bowl. Beat at low speed with electric mixer until blended. Stir in chocolate chips and pecans. Form small amount of dough into 1½-inch ball. Dip top of ball in decors. Place ball decor side up on ungreased baking sheets. Repeat with remaining dough, placing balls 2 inches apart on baking sheets. Bake at 350°F for 10 to 12 minutes or until light golden brown around edges. Cool 2 minutes on baking sheets. Remove to cooling racks. Cool completely. Store in airtight container.

*Makes 3 to 3½ dozen cookies*

**Note:** Cool baking sheet completely before baking each batch of cookies.

## Pinwheel Cookies

½ **cup shortening plus additional for greasing**
⅓ **cup plus 1 tablespoon butter, softened and divided**
 2 **egg yolks**
½ **teaspoon vanilla extract**
 1 **package DUNCAN HINES® Moist Deluxe® Fudge Marble Cake Mix**

**1.** Combine ½ cup shortening, ⅓ cup butter, egg yolks and vanilla extract in large bowl. Mix at low speed of electric mixer until blended. Set aside cocoa packet from cake mix. Gradually add cake mix. Blend well.

**2.** Divide dough in half. Add cocoa packet and remaining 1 tablespoon butter to one half of dough. Knead until well blended and chocolate colored.

**3.** Roll out yellow dough between two pieces of waxed paper into $18\times12\times\frac{1}{8}$-inch rectangle. Repeat for chocolate dough. Remove top pieces of waxed paper from chocolate and yellow doughs. Place yellow dough directly on top of chocolate dough. Remove remaining layers of waxed paper. Roll up jelly-roll fashion, beginning at wide side. Refrigerate 2 hours.

**4.** Preheat oven to 350°F. Grease baking sheets.

**5.** Cut dough into ⅛-inch slices. Place sliced dough 1 inch apart on prepared baking sheets. Bake at 350°F for 9 to 11 minutes or until lightly browned. Cool 5 minutes on baking sheets. Remove to cooling racks.     *Makes about 3½ dozen cookies*

## Butterscotch Spice Cookies

1 package DUNCAN HINES® Moist Deluxe® Spice Cake Mix
2 eggs
½ cup vegetable oil
1 teaspoon vanilla extract
1 cup butterscotch flavored chips

**1.** Preheat oven to 375°F.

**2.** Combine cake mix, eggs, oil and vanilla extract in large bowl. Beat at low speed with electric mixer until blended. Stir in butterscotch chips. Drop by rounded teaspoonfuls 2 inches apart onto ungreased baking sheets. Bake at 375°F for 8 to 10 minutes or until set. Cool 2 minutes on baking sheets. Remove to cooling racks. Cool completely. Store in airtight container.                 *Makes 3 dozen cookies*

**Note:** For chewy cookies, bake for 8 minutes. Cookies will be slightly puffed when removed from the oven and will settle while cooling.

## Easy Lemon Cookies

1 package DUNCAN HINES® Moist Deluxe® Lemon Cake Mix
2 eggs
½ cup vegetable oil
1 teaspoon grated lemon peel
Pecan halves for garnish

**1.** Preheat oven to 350°F.

**2.** Combine cake mix, eggs, oil and lemon peel in large bowl. Stir until thoroughly blended. Drop by rounded teaspoonfuls 2 inches apart onto ungreased baking sheets. Press pecan half into center of each cookie. Bake at 350°F for 9 to 11 minutes or until edges are light golden brown. Cool 1 minute on baking sheets. Remove to wire racks. Cool completely. Store in airtight container.                 *Makes 4 dozen cookies*

**Note:** You can substitute whole almonds or walnut halves for the pecan halves.

## Snickerdoodles

    3 tablespoons sugar
    1 teaspoon ground cinnamon
    1 package DUNCAN HINES® Moist Deluxe® Classic Yellow Cake Mix
    2 eggs
    ¼ cup vegetable oil

**1.** Preheat oven to 375°F. Grease baking sheets. Place sheets of foil on countertop for cooling cookies.

**2.** Combine sugar and cinnamon in small bowl.

**3.** Combine cake mix, eggs and oil in large bowl. Stir until well blended. Shape dough into 1-inch balls. Roll in cinnamon-sugar mixture. Place balls 2 inches apart on prepared baking sheets. Flatten balls with bottom of glass.

**4.** Bake at 375°F for 8 to 9 minutes or until set. Cool 1 minute on baking sheets. Remove to foil to cool completely.                    ***Makes about 3 dozen cookies***

## Vanilla Butter Crescents

    1 package DUNCAN HINES® Moist Deluxe® French Vanilla Cake Mix
    ¾ cup butter, softened
    1 vanilla bean, very finely chopped (see Hint)
    1 cup finely chopped pecans or walnuts
       Confectioners' sugar

**1.** Preheat oven to 350°F.

**2.** Place cake mix and butter in large bowl. Cut in butter with pastry blender or 2 knives. Stir in vanilla bean and pecans. Since mixture is crumbly, it may be helpful to work dough with hands to blend until mixture holds together. Shape dough into balls. Roll 1 ball between palms until 4 inches long. Shape into crescent. Repeat with remaining balls. Place 2 inches apart on ungreased baking sheets. Bake at 350°F for 10 to 12 minutes or until light golden brown around edges. Cool 2 minutes on baking sheets. Remove to cooling racks. Dust with confectioners' sugar. Cool completely. Dust with additional confectioners' sugar, if desired. Store in airtight container.

***Makes 4 dozen cookies***

**Hint:** To quickly chop vanilla bean, place in work bowl of food processor fitted with knife blade. Process until fine.

## Double Nut Chocolate Chip Cookies

1 package DUNCAN HINES® Moist Deluxe® Classic Yellow Cake Mix
½ cup butter or margarine, melted
1 egg
1 cup semisweet chocolate chips
½ cup finely chopped pecans
1 cup sliced almonds, divided

**1.** Preheat oven to 375°F. Grease baking sheets.

**2.** Combine cake mix, butter and egg in large bowl. Mix at low speed with electric mixer until just blended. Stir in chocolate chips, pecans and ¼ cup almonds. Shape rounded tablespoonfuls of dough into balls. Place remaining ¾ cup almonds in shallow bowl. Press tops of cookies into almonds. Place 1 inch apart on prepared baking sheets.

**3.** Bake at 375°F for 9 to 11 minutes or until lightly browned. Cool 2 minutes on baking sheets. Remove to cooling racks. *Makes 3 to 3½ dozen cookies*

## Spicy Sour Cream Cookies

1 package DUNCAN HINES® Moist Deluxe® Spice Cake Mix
1 cup sour cream
1 cup chopped pecans or walnuts
¼ cup butter or margarine, softened
1 egg

**1.** Preheat oven to 350°F. Grease baking sheets.

**2.** Combine cake mix, sour cream, pecans, butter and egg in large bowl. Mix at low speed with electric mixer until blended.

**3.** Drop dough by rounded teaspoonfuls onto prepared baking sheets. Bake at 350°F for 9 to 11 minutes or until lightly browned. Cool 2 minutes on baking sheets. Remove to cooling racks; cool completely. *Makes about 4½ dozen cookies*

## Cinnamon Stars

2 tablespoons sugar
¾ teaspoon ground cinnamon
¾ cup butter or margarine, softened
2 egg yolks
1 teaspoon vanilla extract
1 package DUNCAN HINES® Moist Deluxe® French Vanilla Cake Mix

**1.** Preheat oven to 375°F. Combine sugar and cinnamon in small bowl. Set aside.

**2.** Combine butter, egg yolks and vanilla extract in large bowl. Blend in cake mix gradually. Roll dough to ⅛-inch thickness on lightly floured surface. Cut with 2½-inch star cookie cutter. Place 2 inches apart on ungreased baking sheet.

**3.** Sprinkle cookies with cinnamon-sugar mixture. Bake at 375°F for 6 to 8 minutes or until edges are light golden brown. Cool 1 minute on baking sheet. Remove to cooling rack. Cool completely. Store in airtight container.

*Makes 3 to 3½ dozen cookies*

**Note:** You can use your favorite cookie cutter in place of the star cookie cutter.

### Tip

For even baking and browning of cookies, place only one baking sheet at a time in the center of the oven. Allow at least two inches of space between the baking sheet and the wall of the oven for proper air circulation. If the cookies brown unevenly, rotate the baking sheet from front to back halfway through the baking time.

## Chocolate Oat Chewies

    1 package DUNCAN HINES® Moist Deluxe® Devil's Food Cake Mix
1⅓ cups old-fashioned oats, uncooked
    1 cup flaked coconut, toasted and divided
    ¾ cup butter or margarine, melted
    2 eggs, beaten
    1 teaspoon vanilla extract
    5 bars (1.55 ounces each) milk chocolate, cut into rectangles

**1.** Preheat oven to 350°F.

**2.** Combine cake mix, oats, ½ cup coconut, butter, eggs and vanilla extract in large bowl. Cover and chill 15 minutes.

**3.** Shape dough into 1-inch balls. Place balls 2 inches apart on ungreased baking sheets. Bake at 350°F for 12 minutes or until tops are slightly cracked. Remove from oven. Press one milk chocolate rectangle into center of each cookie. Sprinkle with remaining ½ cup coconut. Remove to cooling racks.

*Makes about 4½ dozen cookies*

## Quick Peanut Butter Chocolate Chip Cookies

    1 package DUNCAN HINES® Moist Deluxe® Classic Yellow Cake Mix
    ½ cup creamy peanut butter
    ½ cup butter or margarine, softened
    2 eggs
    1 cup milk chocolate chips

**1.** Preheat oven to 350°F. Grease baking sheets.

**2.** Combine cake mix, peanut butter, butter and eggs in large bowl. Mix at low speed with electric mixer until blended. Stir in chocolate chips.

**3.** Drop by rounded teaspoonfuls onto prepared baking sheets. Bake at 350°F for 9 to 11 minutes or until lightly browned. Cool 2 minutes on baking sheets. Remove to cooling racks.

*Makes about 4 dozen cookies*

**Note:** Crunchy peanut butter can be substituted for regular peanut butter.

## Lemon Cookies

1 package DUNCAN HINES® Moist Deluxe® Lemon Supreme Cake Mix
2 eggs
⅓ cup vegetable oil
1 tablespoon lemon juice
¾ cup chopped nuts or flaked coconut
Confectioners' sugar

**1.** Preheat oven to 375°F. Grease baking sheets.

**2.** Combine cake mix, eggs, oil and lemon juice in large bowl. Beat at low speed with electric mixer until well blended. Add nuts. Shape dough into 1-inch balls. Place 1 inch apart on prepared baking sheets.

**3.** Bake at 375°F for 6 to 7 minutes or until lightly browned. Cool 1 minute on baking sheets. Remove to cooling racks. Sprinkle with confectioners' sugar.

*Makes about 3 dozen cookies*

**Hint:** You can frost cookies with 1 cup confectioners' sugar mixed with 1 tablespoon lemon juice instead of sprinkling cookies with confectioners' sugar.

### Tip

Before dusting cookies with confectioners' sugar or drizzling them with chocolate or icing, place waxed paper under the wire rack to make cleanup easier.

## Spicy Oatmeal Raisin Cookies

1 package DUNCAN HINES® Moist Deluxe® Spice Cake Mix
4 egg whites
1 cup uncooked quick-cooking oats (not instant or old-fashioned)
½ cup vegetable oil
½ cup raisins

**1.** Preheat oven to 350°F. Grease baking sheets.

**2.** Combine cake mix, egg whites, oats and oil in large mixing bowl. Beat at low speed with electric mixer until blended. Stir in raisins. Drop by rounded teaspoonfuls onto prepared baking sheets.

**3.** Bake at 350°F for 7 to 9 minutes or until lightly browned. Cool 1 minute on baking sheets. Remove to cooling racks; cool completely.

*Makes about 4 dozen cookies*

## Cinnamon Crinkles

2 tablespoons sugar
½ teaspoon ground cinnamon
2 eggs, separated
1 teaspoon water
¾ cup butter or margarine, softened
1 teaspoon vanilla extract
1 package DUNCAN HINES® Moist Deluxe® French Vanilla Cake Mix
48 whole almonds or pecan halves for garnish

**1.** Preheat oven to 375°F. Combine sugar and cinnamon in small bowl. Set aside. Combine egg whites and water in another small bowl; beat lightly with fork. Set aside.

**2.** Combine butter, egg yolks and vanilla extract in large bowl. Blend in cake mix gradually. Beat at low speed with electric mixer until blended. Roll 1 rounded teaspoon of dough into ball. Dip half the ball into egg white mixture then into cinnamon-sugar mixture. Place ball sugar side up on ungreased baking sheet. Press almond on top. Repeat with remaining dough, placing balls 2 inches apart.

**3.** Bake at 375°F for 9 to 12 minutes or until edges are light golden brown. Cool 2 minutes on baking sheets. Remove to cooling racks. Store in airtight container.

*Makes 4 dozen cookies*

**Note:** Cookies will be slightly puffed when removed from the oven and will settle during cooling.

# Tasty Brownies & Bars

## Scrumptious Minted Brownies

**1 package (21 ounces) DUNCAN HINES® Family-Style Chewy Fudge Brownie Mix**
**1 egg**
**⅓ cup water**
**⅓ cup vegetable oil**
**48 chocolate crème de menthe candy wafers, divided**

**1.** Preheat oven to 350°F. Grease bottom only of 13×9-inch pan.

**2.** Combine brownie mix, egg, water and oil in large bowl. Stir with spoon until well blended, about 50 strokes. Spread in prepared pan. Bake at 350°F for 25 minutes or until set. Place 30 candy wafers evenly over hot brownies. Let stand for 1 minute to melt. Spread candy wafers to frost brownies. Score frosting into 36 bars by running tip of knife through melted candy. (Do not cut through brownies.) Cut remaining 18 candy wafers in half lengthwise; place halves on each scored bar. Cool completely. Cut into bars.          ***Makes 36 brownies***

## Sweet Walnut Maple Bars

*Crust*

    1 package DUNCAN HINES® Moist Deluxe® Classic Yellow Cake Mix, divided

    $\frac{1}{3}$ cup butter or margarine, melted

    1 egg

*Topping*

    $1\frac{1}{3}$ cups MRS. BUTTERWORTH'S® Maple Syrup

    3 eggs

    $\frac{1}{3}$ cup firmly packed light brown sugar

    $\frac{1}{2}$ teaspoon maple flavoring or vanilla extract

    1 cup chopped walnuts

**1.** Preheat oven to 350°F. Grease 13×9×2-inch pan.

**2.** For crust, reserve $\frac{2}{3}$ cup cake mix; set aside. Combine remaining cake mix, melted butter and egg in large bowl. Stir until thoroughly blended. (Mixture will be crumbly.) Press into prepared pan. Bake at 350°F for 15 to 20 minutes or until light golden brown.

**3.** For topping, combine reserved cake mix, maple syrup, eggs, brown sugar and maple flavoring in large bowl. Beat at low speed with electric mixer for 3 minutes. Pour over crust. Sprinkle with walnuts. Bake at 350°F for 30 to 35 minutes or until filling is set. Cool completely. Cut into bars. Store leftover cookie bars in refrigerator.

*Makes 24 bars*

## Double Chocolate Chewies

1 package DUNCAN HINES® Moist Deluxe® Butter Recipe Fudge Cake
   Mix
2 eggs
½ cup butter or margarine, melted
1 package (6 ounces) semisweet chocolate chips
1 cup chopped nuts
   Confectioners' sugar (optional)

**1.** Preheat oven to 350°F. Grease 13×9×2-inch pan.

**2.** Combine cake mix, eggs and melted butter in large bowl. Stir until thoroughly blended. (Mixture will be stiff.) Stir in chocolate chips and nuts. Press mixture evenly in prepared pan. Bake at 350°F for 25 to 30 minutes or until toothpick inserted in center comes out clean. *Do not overbake.* Cool completely. Cut into bars. Dust with confectioners' sugar, if desired. *Makes 36 bars*

## Butter Fudge Fingers

1 package (21 ounces) DUNCAN HINES® Family-Style Chewy Fudge
   Brownie Mix
1 container DUNCAN HINES® Creamy Home-Style Buttercream
   Frosting
¼ cup semisweet chocolate chips
1½ teaspoons shortening plus additional for greasing

**1.** Preheat oven to 350°F. Grease bottom only of 13×9×2-inch pan.

**2.** Prepare, bake and cool brownies following package directions for basic recipe chewy brownies. Spread with Buttercream frosting.

**3.** Place chocolate chips and shortening in small resealable plastic bag; seal. Microwave at HIGH (100% power) 30 seconds, adding 15 to 30 seconds more if needed. Knead until blended. Snip pinpoint hole in corner of bag. Drizzle chocolate over frosting. Allow chocolate to set before cutting into bars. *Makes 18 brownies*

**Hint:** Another method for melting the chocolate and shortening in the sealed bag is to place it in a bowl of hot water for several minutes. Dry the bag with a paper towel. Knead, snip and pipe as directed above.

Double Chocolate Chewies

## Fudgy Hazelnut Brownies

**1 package (21 ounces) DUNCAN HINES® Chewy Fudge Brownie Mix**
**2 eggs**
**½ cup vegetable oil**
**¼ cup water**
**1 cup chopped toasted hazelnuts**
**1 cup semisweet chocolate chips**
**1 cup DUNCAN HINES® Dark Chocolate Frosting**
**3 squares white chocolate, melted**

**1.** Preheat oven to 350°F. Grease bottom only of 13×9-inch baking pan.

**2.** Combine brownie mix, eggs, oil and water in large bowl. Stir with spoon until well blended, about 50 strokes. Stir in hazelnuts and chocolate chips. Spread in prepared pan. Bake at 350°F for 25 to 30 minutes or until set. Cool completely.

**3.** Heat frosting in microwave oven at HIGH for 15 seconds or until thin; stir well. Spread over brownies. Spoon dollops of white chocolate over chocolate frosting; marble white chocolate through frosting. Cool completely. Cut into bars.

*Makes 24 brownies*

### Tip

Toasting nuts before using them intensifies their flavor and crunch. To toast nuts, spread them on a baking sheet and place in a 350°F oven for 8 to 10 minutes. Always cool nuts to room temperature before combining them with other ingredients.

## Lemon Bars

1 package DUNCAN HINES® Moist Deluxe® Lemon Supreme Cake Mix
3 eggs, divided
$\frac{1}{3}$ cup butter-flavor shortening
$\frac{1}{2}$ cup granulated sugar
$\frac{1}{4}$ cup lemon juice
2 teaspoons grated lemon peel
$\frac{1}{2}$ teaspoon baking powder
$\frac{1}{4}$ teaspoon salt
Confectioners' sugar

**1.** Preheat oven to 350°F.

**2.** Combine cake mix, 1 egg and shortening in large mixing bowl. Beat at low speed with electric mixer until crumbs form. Reserve 1 cup. Pat remaining mixture lightly into ungreased 13×9-inch pan. Bake at 350°F for 15 minutes or until lightly browned.

**3.** Combine remaining 2 eggs, granulated sugar, lemon juice, lemon peel, baking powder and salt in medium mixing bowl. Beat at medium speed with electric mixer until light and foamy. Pour over hot crust. Sprinkle with reserved crumb mixture.

**4.** Bake at 350°F for 15 minutes or until lightly browned. Sprinkle with confectioners' sugar. Cool in pan. Cut into bars. *Makes 30 to 32 bars*

**Hint:** These bars are also delicious using Duncan Hines® Moist Deluxe® Classic Yellow Cake Mix.

## Butterscotch Pan Cookies

　　1 package DUNCAN HINES® Moist Deluxe® French Vanilla Cake Mix
　　2 eggs
　　1 cup butter or margarine, melted
　¾ cup firmly packed light brown sugar
　　1 teaspoon vanilla extract
　　1 package (12 ounces) butterscotch flavored chips
1½ cups chopped pecans

**1.** Preheat oven to 375°F. Grease 15½×10½×1-inch jelly-roll pan.

**2.** Combine cake mix, eggs, melted butter, brown sugar and vanilla extract in large bowl. Beat at low speed with electric mixer until smooth and creamy. Stir in butterscotch chips and pecans. Spread in prepared pan. Bake at 375°F for 20 to 25 minutes or until golden brown. Cool completely. Cut into bars.

*Makes 48 bars*

**Hint:** You can substitute chocolate or peanut butter flavored chips for the butterscotch flavored chips.

## Marshmallow Krispie Bars

　　1 package (21 ounces) DUNCAN HINES® Family-Style Chewy Fudge
　　　　Brownie Mix
　　1 package (10½ ounces) miniature marshmallows
1½ cups semisweet chocolate chips
　　1 cup creamy peanut butter
　　1 tablespoon butter or margarine
1½ cups crisp rice cereal

**1.** Preheat oven to 350°F. Grease bottom only of 13×9-inch pan.

**2.** Prepare and bake brownies following package directions for cake-like recipe. Remove from oven. Sprinkle marshmallows on hot brownies. Return to oven. Bake for 3 minutes longer.

**3.** Place chocolate chips, peanut butter and butter in medium saucepan. Cook over low heat, stirring constantly, until chips are melted. Add rice cereal; mix well. Spread mixture over marshmallow layer. Refrigerate until chilled. Cut into bars.

*Makes about 2 dozen bars*

## Orange Chess Bars

*Crust*
> **1 package DUNCAN HINES® Moist Deluxe® Orange Supreme Cake Mix**
> **½ cup vegetable oil**
> **⅓ cup chopped pecans**

*Topping*
> **1 pound (3½ to 4 cups) confectioners' sugar**
> **1 package (8 ounces) cream cheese, softened**
> **2 eggs**
> **2 teaspoons grated orange peel**

**1.** Preheat oven to 350°F. Grease 13×9-inch baking pan.

**2.** For crust, combine cake mix, oil and pecans in large bowl. Stir until blended (mixture will be crumbly). Press in bottom of prepared pan.

**3.** For topping, combine confectioners' sugar and cream cheese in large bowl. Beat at low speed with electric mixer until blended. Add eggs and orange peel. Beat at low speed until blended. Pour over crust. Bake at 350°F for 30 to 35 minutes or until topping is set. Cool. Refrigerate until ready to serve. Cut into bars.

***Makes about 24 bars***

## Mississippi Mud Brownies

> **1 package (21 ounces) DUNCAN HINES® Family-Style Chewy Fudge Brownie Mix**
> **2 eggs**
> **⅓ cup water**
> **⅓ cup vegetable oil plus additional for greasing**
> **1 jar (7 ounces) marshmallow creme**
> **1 container DUNCAN HINES® Milk Chocolate Frosting, melted**

**1.** Preheat oven to 350°F. Grease bottom only of 13×9-inch pan.

**2.** Combine brownie mix, eggs, water and oil in large bowl. Stir with spoon until well blended, about 50 strokes. Spread evenly in prepared pan. Bake at 350°F for 25 to 28 minutes or until set.

**3.** Spread marshmallow creme gently over hot brownies. Pour 1¼ cups melted Milk Chocolate frosting over marshmallow creme. Swirl with knife to marble. Cool completely. Cut into bars.

***Makes 20 to 24 brownies***

**Note:** Store leftover melted frosting in original container. Refrigerate.

## Cindy's Fudgy Brownies

**1 package (21 ounces) DUNCAN HINES® Family-Style Chewy Fudge Brownie Mix**
**1 egg**
**⅓ cup water**
**⅓ cup vegetable oil**
**¾ cup semisweet chocolate chips**
**½ cup chopped pecans**

**1.** Preheat oven to 350°F. Grease bottom only of 13×9×2-inch pan.

**2.** Combine brownie mix, egg, water and oil in large bowl. Stir with spoon until well blended, about 50 strokes. Stir in chocolate chips. Spread in prepared pan. Sprinkle with pecans. Bake at 350°F for 25 to 28 minutes or until set. Cool completely. Cut into bars.          *Makes 24 brownies*

**Note:** Overbaking brownies will cause them to become dry. Follow the recommended baking times given in recipes closely.

---

### Tip

When baking brownies, always use the pan size called for in the recipe. Substituting a different pan will affect their texture as well as the baking time. A smaller pan will give the brownies a more cakelike texture; a larger pan will produce flatter brownies with a drier texture.

---

## Blueberry Cheesecake Bars

1 package DUNCAN HINES® Bakery-Style Blueberry Streusel Muffin
    Mix
¼ cup cold butter or margarine
⅓ cup finely chopped pecans
1 package (8 ounces) cream cheese, softened
½ cup sugar
1 egg
3 tablespoons lemon juice
1 teaspoon grated lemon peel

**1.** Preheat oven to 350°F. Grease 9-inch square baking pan.

**2.** Rinse blueberries from Mix with cold water and drain.

**3.** Place muffin mix in medium bowl; cut in butter with pastry blender or two knives. Stir in pecans. Press into bottom of prepared pan. Bake at 350°F for 15 minutes or until set.

**4.** Combine cream cheese and sugar in medium bowl. Beat until smooth. Add egg, lemon juice and lemon peel. Beat well. Spread over baked crust. Sprinkle with blueberries. Sprinkle topping packet from Mix over blueberries. Return to oven. Bake at 350°F for 35 to 40 minutes or until filling is set. Cool completely. Refrigerate until ready to serve. Cut into bars. *Makes about 16 bars*

## Macaroon Brownies

1 package (21 ounces) DUNCAN HINES® Family-Style Chewy Fudge
    Brownie Mix
2 egg whites
½ cup granulated sugar
¼ teaspoon almond extract
1 cup finely chopped almonds
1 cup flaked coconut

**1.** Preheat oven to 350°F. Grease bottom only of 13×9-inch pan.

**2.** Prepare brownies as directed on package for cake-like brownies. Bake at 350°F for 25 minutes or until set. Place egg whites in medium mixing bowl. Beat at high speed with electric mixer until foamy and double in volume. Beat in sugar gradually, beating until meringue forms firm peaks. Add almond extract. Fold in almonds and coconut. Spread over warm brownies. Bake at 350°F for 12 to 14 minutes or until meringue is set and lightly browned. Cool completely. Cut into bars. *Makes 24 brownies*

Blueberry Cheesecake Bars

## Double Mint Brownies

1 package (21 ounces) DUNCAN HINES® Family-Style Chewy Recipe
     Fudge Brownie Mix
1 egg
⅓ cup water
⅓ cup vegetable oil plus additional for greasing
½ teaspoon peppermint extract
24 chocolate-covered peppermint patties (1½ inches each)
1 cup confectioners' sugar, divided
4 teaspoons milk, divided
   Red food coloring
   Green food coloring

**1.** Preheat oven to 350°F. Grease bottom only of 13×9×2-inch pan. Combine brownie mix, egg, water, oil and peppermint extract in large bowl. Stir with spoon until well blended, about 50 strokes. Spread in prepared pan. Bake brownies following package directions. Place peppermint patties on warm brownies. Cool completely.

**2.** Combine ½ cup confectioners' sugar, 2 teaspoons milk and 1 drop red food coloring in small bowl. Stir until smooth. Place in small resealable plastic bag; set aside. Repeat with remaining ½ cup confectioners' sugar, remaining 2 teaspoons milk and 1 drop green food coloring. Cut pinpoint hole in bottom corner of each bag. Drizzle pink and green glazes over brownies as shown. Allow glazes to set before cutting into bars.                               *Makes 24 brownies*

**Hint:** To prevent overdone edges and an underdone center, wrap foil strips around the outside edges of the pan (do not cover the bottom or the top). Bake as directed above.

**Double Mint Brownies**

## Pecan Date Bars

*Crust*

    ⅓ cup shortening plus additional for greasing
    1 package DUNCAN HINES® Moist Deluxe® Classic White Cake Mix
    1 egg

*Topping*

    1 package (8 ounces) chopped dates
  1¼ cups chopped pecans
    1 cup water
    ½ teaspoon vanilla extract
    Confectioners' sugar

**1.** Preheat oven to 350°F. Grease and flour 13×9-inch baking pan.

**2.** For crust, cut ⅓ cup shortening into cake mix with pastry blender or 2 knives until mixture resembles coarse crumbs. Add egg; stir well (mixture will be crumbly). Press mixture into bottom of prepared pan.

**3.** For topping, combine dates, pecans and water in medium saucepan. Bring to a boil. Reduce heat; simmer until mixture thickens, stirring constantly. Remove from heat. Stir in vanilla extract. Spread date mixture evenly over crust. Bake at 350°F for 25 to 30 minutes. Cool completely. Dust with confectioners' sugar.

*Makes about 32 bars*

### Tip

Most bar cookies should cool in the pan on a wire rack until barely warm before cutting them into bars or squares. Try cutting bar cookies into triangles or diamonds for a festive new shape. To make serving easy, remove a corner piece first; then remove the rest.

## Toffee Brownie Bars

*Crust*
   ¾ cup butter or margarine, softened
   ¾ cup firmly packed brown sugar
    1 egg yolk
   ¾ teaspoon vanilla extract
  1½ cups all-purpose flour

*Filling*
    1 package (21 ounces) DUNCAN HINES® Family-Style Chewy Fudge
        Brownie Mix
    1 egg
   ⅓ cup water
   ⅓ cup vegetable oil

*Topping*
    1 package (12 ounces) milk chocolate chips, melted
   ¾ cup finely chopped pecans

**1.** Preheat oven to 350°F. Grease 15½×10½×1-inch pan.

**2.** For crust, combine butter, brown sugar, egg yolk and vanilla extract in large bowl. Stir in flour. Spread in prepared pan. Bake at 350°F for 15 minutes or until golden.

**3.** For filling, prepare brownie mix following package directions. Spread over hot crust. Bake at 350°F for 15 minutes or until surface appears set. Cool 30 minutes.

**4.** For topping, spread melted chocolate on top of brownie layer; sprinkle with pecans. Cool completely. *Makes 48 bars*

**Note:** Bars can be made ahead and frozen in an airtight container for several weeks.

# *Breakfast Sweets*

## Orange Cinnamon Swirl Bread

*Bread*
> 1 package DUNCAN HINES® Bakery-Style Cinnamon Swirl Muffin Mix
> 1 egg
> $^2/_3$ cup orange juice
> 1 tablespoon grated orange peel

*Orange Glaze*
> $^1/_2$ cup confectioners' sugar
> 2 to 3 teaspoons orange juice
> 1 teaspoon grated orange peel
> Quartered orange slices for garnish (optional)

**1.** Preheat oven to 350°F. Grease and flour $8^1/_2 \times 4^1/_2 \times 2^1/_2$-inch loaf pan.

**2.** For bread, combine muffin mix and contents of topping packet from mix in large bowl. Break up any lumps. Add egg, $^2/_3$ cup orange juice and 1 tablespoon orange peel. Stir until moistened, about 50 strokes. Knead swirl packet from mix for 10 seconds before opening. Squeeze contents on top of batter. Swirl into batter with knife or spatula, folding from bottom of bowl to get an even swirl. *Do not completely mix in.* Pour into prepared pan. Bake at 350°F for 55 to 60 minutes or until toothpick inserted in center comes out clean. Cool in pan 10 minutes. Loosen loaf from pan. Invert onto cooling rack. Turn right side up. Cool.

**3.** For orange glaze, place confectioners' sugar in small bowl. Add orange juice, 1 teaspoon at a time, stirring until smooth and of desired consistency. Stir in 1 teaspoon orange peel. Drizzle over loaf. Garnish with orange slices, if desired.

*Makes 1 loaf (12 slices)*

## Nutty Blueberry Muffins

**1 package DUNCAN HINES® Bakery-Style Wild Maine Blueberry**
**Muffin Mix**
**2 egg whites**
**½ cup water**
**⅓ cup chopped pecans**

**1.** Preheat oven to 400°F. Grease 2½-inch muffin cups (or use paper liners).

**2.** Rinse blueberries from Mix with cold water and drain.

**3.** Pour muffin mix into large bowl. Break up any lumps. Add egg whites and water. Stir until moistened, about 50 strokes. Stir in pecans; fold in blueberries.

**4.** For large muffins, fill cups two-thirds full. Bake at 400°F for 17 to 22 minutes or until toothpick inserted in centers comes out clean. (For medium muffins, fill cups half full. Bake at 400°F for 15 to 20 minutes.) Cool in pan 5 to 10 minutes. Loosen carefully before removing from pan.     *Makes 8 large or 12 medium muffins*

**Note:** To reheat leftover muffins, wrap the muffins tightly in foil. Place them in a 400°F oven for 10 to 15 minutes.

### Tip

Don't stir muffin batter too much–overmixing will make the muffins tough. There should still be lumps in the batter; these will disappear during baking.

## Cranberry Pecan Muffins

1½ cups fresh or frozen cranberries
¼ cup light corn syrup
1 package DUNCAN HINES® Bakery-Style Cinnamon Swirl Muffin Mix
1 egg
¾ cup water or milk
½ cup chopped pecans

**1.** Preheat oven to 400°F. Place 14 (2½-inch) paper liners in muffin cups. Place cranberries and corn syrup in heavy saucepan. Cook on medium heat, stirring occasionally, until cranberries pop and mixture is slightly thickened. Drain cranberries in strainer; set aside.

**2.** Empty muffin mix into medium bowl. Break up any lumps. Add egg and water. Stir until moistened, about 50 strokes. Stir in cranberries and pecans. Knead swirl packet from Mix for 10 seconds before opening. Cut off 1 end of swirl packet. Squeeze contents over top of batter. Swirl into batter with knife or spatula. *Do not completely mix in.* Spoon batter into muffin cups (see Note). Sprinkle with contents of topping packet from Mix. Bake at 400°F for 18 to 22 minutes or until toothpick inserted into centers comes out clean. Cool in pans 5 to 10 minutes. Serve warm or cool completely.

*Makes 14 muffins*

**Note:** Fill an equal number of muffin cups in each muffin pan with batter. For more even baking, fill empty muffin cups with ½ inch of water.

## Coconut Chocolate Chip Loaf

1 package DUNCAN HINES® Bakery-Style Chocolate Chip Muffin Mix
1⅓ cups toasted flaked coconut (see Note)
1 egg
¾ cup water
½ teaspoon vanilla extract
Confectioners' sugar for garnish (optional)

**1.** Preheat oven to 350°F. Grease and flour 9×5×3-inch loaf pan.

**2.** Empty muffin mix into medium bowl. Break up any lumps. Add coconut, egg, water and vanilla extract. Stir until moistened, about 50 strokes. Pour into prepared pan. Bake at 350°F for 45 to 50 minutes or until toothpick inserted in center comes out clean. Cool in pan 15 minutes. Invert onto cooling rack. Turn right side up. Cool completely. Dust with confectioners' sugar, if desired.     *Makes 1 loaf (12 slices)*

**Note:** Spread coconut evenly on baking sheet. Toast at 350°F for 5 minutes. Stir and toast 1 to 2 minutes longer or until light golden brown.

## Golden Oatmeal Muffins

1 package DUNCAN HINES® Moist Deluxe® Butter Recipe Golden Cake Mix
1 cup uncooked quick-cooking oats (not instant or old-fashioned)
¼ teaspoon salt
¾ cup milk
2 eggs, lightly beaten
2 tablespoons butter or margarine, melted

**1.** Preheat oven to 400°F. Grease 24 (2½-inch) muffin cups (or use paper liners).

**2.** Combine cake mix, oats and salt in large bowl. Add milk, eggs and melted butter; stir until moistened. Fill muffin cups two-thirds full. Bake at 400°F for 13 minutes or until golden brown. Cool in pan 5 to 10 minutes. Loosen carefully before removing from pan. Serve with honey or your favorite jam.     *Makes 2 dozen muffins*

## Orange Pecan Brunch Cake

1 package DUNCAN HINES® Moist Deluxe® Orange Supreme Cake Mix
3 eggs
⅔ cup dairy sour cream
½ cup water
⅓ cup chopped pecans
⅓ cup vegetable oil
2 tablespoons lemon juice
1 teaspoon ground cinnamon
Mandarin orange segments
Strawberry slices
Kiwifruit slices
½ cup apricot preserves, heated and strained
Mint leaves for garnish (optional)

**1.** Preheat oven to 350°F. Grease and flour 10-inch Bundt or tube pan.

**2.** Combine cake mix, eggs, sour cream, water, pecans, oil, lemon juice and cinnamon in large bowl. Beat at low speed with electric mixer until moistened. Beat at medium speed for 2 minutes. Pour into prepared pan. Bake at 350°F for 48 to 53 minutes or until toothpick inserted in center comes out clean. Cool in pan 25 minutes. Invert onto serving plate.

**3.** Dry fruit thoroughly between layers of paper towels. Arrange fruit pieces on top of cake. Brush with warmed preserves. Drizzle remaining preserves over top and sides of cake. Garnish with mint leaves, if desired. Serve warm or cool completely and refrigerate until ready to serve. *Makes 12 to 16 servings*

**Hint:** For a different presentation, brush the cake with warmed preserves and serve your favorite fruit assortment on the side.

## Cinnamon Twists

*Rolls*

    1 package DUNCAN HINES® Bakery-Style Cinnamon Swirl Muffin Mix, divided

    2 cups all-purpose flour

    1 package (¼ ounce) quick-rise yeast

    1 egg, lightly beaten

    1 cup hot water (120° to 130°F)

    2 tablespoons butter or margarine, melted

    1 egg white, lightly beaten

    1 teaspoon water

*Topping*

    1½ cups confectioners' sugar

    2½ tablespoons milk

**1.** Grease 2 large baking sheets.

**2.** For rolls, combine muffin mix, flour and yeast in large bowl; set aside.

**3.** Combine contents of swirl packet from Mix, egg, hot water and melted butter in medium bowl. Stir until thoroughly blended. Pour into flour mixture; stir until thoroughly blended. Invert onto well-floured surface; let rest for 10 minutes. Knead for 10 minutes or until smooth, adding flour as necessary. Divide dough in half. Cut and shape 24 small ropes from each half. Braid 3 ropes to form small twist and place on greased baking sheet. Combine egg white and 1 teaspoon water in small bowl. Brush each twist with egg white mixture and sprinkle with contents of topping packet from Mix. Allow twists to rise 1 hour or until doubled in size.

**4.** Preheat oven to 375°F.

**5.** Bake twists at 375°F for 17 to 20 minutes or until deep golden brown. Remove to cooling racks.

**6.** For topping, combine confectioners' sugar and milk in small bowl. Stir until smooth. Drizzle over warm rolls. Serve warm or cool completely.

*Makes 16 rolls*

**Note:** For best results, let rolls rise in a warm, draft-free area. A slightly warm oven (130° to 140°F) is ideal.

## Berry Filled Muffins

1 package **DUNCAN HINES®** **Bakery-Style Wild Maine Blueberry**
   **Muffin Mix**
1 **egg**
½ **cup water**
¼ **cup strawberry jam**
2 **tablespoons sliced natural almonds**

**1.** Preheat oven to 400°F. Place 8 (2½-inch) paper or foil liners in muffin cups; set aside.

**2.** Rinse blueberries from Mix with cold water and drain.

**3.** Empty muffin mix into bowl. Break up any lumps. Add egg and water. Stir until moistened, about 50 strokes. Fill cups half full with batter.

**4.** Fold blueberries into jam. Spoon on top of batter in each cup. Spread gently. Cover with remaining batter. Sprinkle with almonds. Bake at 400°F for 17 to 20 minutes or until set and golden brown. Cool in pan 5 to 10 minutes. Loosen carefully before removing from pan.                    *Makes 8 muffins*

**Hint:** For a delicious flavor variation, try using blackberry or red raspberry jam instead of the strawberry jam.

### Tip

When baking muffins, pour water into any empty muffin cups to prevent the muffin pan from warping in the oven. Muffins are done when the center springs back when lightly touched and a toothpick inserted into the center comes out clean and dry.

## Yeasty Cinnamon Loaves

1 package DUNCAN HINES® Bakery-Style Cinnamon Swirl Muffin Mix, divided
5 cups all-purpose flour
2 packages (¼ ounce each) quick-rise yeast
2 eggs, lightly beaten
¼ cup plus 2 tablespoons butter or margarine, melted, divided
2½ cups hot water (120° to 130°F), divided

**1.** Grease two 9×5×3-inch loaf pans.

**2.** Combine muffin mix, contents of crumb topping from Mix, flour and yeast in large bowl; set aside.

**3.** Combine contents of swirl packet from Mix, eggs, ¼ cup melted butter and ½ cup hot water in medium bowl. Stir well. Add remaining 2 cups hot water and stir until thoroughly blended. Add liquid ingredients to flour mixture; stir until thoroughly blended. Invert onto well-floured surface; let rest for 10 minutes. Knead for 10 minutes or until smooth, adding flour as necessary. Divide dough in half. Divide each half into 3 sections. Roll each section into 10-inch rope. Braid 3 ropes. Fold ends under. Place in greased pan. Repeat with remaining dough. Let rise 1 hour or until doubled in size.

**4.** Preheat oven to 375°F.

**5.** Bake loaves at 375°F for 30 to 35 minutes or until bread is deep golden brown and sounds hollow when tapped. Brush with remaining 2 tablespoons melted butter. Cool in pans 5 minutes. Remove bread from pans to cooling racks. Cool completely.

*Makes 2 loaves*

**Note:** You can also braid loaves and bake free-form on greased baking sheets for 26 to 30 minutes.

**From top to bottom: Yeasty Cinnamon Loaf and Cinnamon Twists (page 55)**

## Blueberry Orange Muffins

**1 package DUNCAN HINES® Bakery-Style Wild Maine Blueberry
Muffin Mix**
**½ cup orange juice**
**2 egg whites**
**1 teaspoon grated orange peel**

**1.** Preheat oven to 400°F. Grease 2½-inch muffin cups (or use paper liners).

**2.** Rinse blueberries from Mix with cold water and drain.

**3.** Empty muffin mix into large bowl. Break up any lumps. Add orange juice, egg whites and orange peel. Stir until moistened, about 50 strokes. Fold blueberries gently into batter.

**4.** For large muffins, fill cups two-thirds full. Bake at 400°F for 18 to 21 minutes or until toothpick inserted into centers comes out clean. (For medium muffins, fill cups half full. Bake at 400°F for 16 to 19 minutes or until toothpick inserted into centers comes out clean.) Cool in pan 5 to 10 minutes. Carefully loosen muffins from pan. Remove to cooling racks. Serve warm or cool completely.

*Makes 8 large or 12 medium muffins*

**Hint:** Freeze extra grated orange peel for future use.

## Peachy Cinnamon Coffeecake

1 can (8¼ ounces) juice packed sliced yellow cling peaches
1 package DUNCAN HINES® Bakery-Style Cinnamon Swirl Muffin Mix
1 egg

**1.** Preheat oven to 400°F. Grease 8-inch square or 9-inch round pan.

**2.** Drain peaches, reserving juice. Add water to reserved juice to equal ¾ cup liquid. Chop peaches.

**3.** Combine muffin mix, egg and ¾ cup peach liquid in medium bowl; fold in peaches. Pour batter into prepared pan. Knead swirl packet 10 seconds before opening. Squeeze contents onto top of batter and swirl with knife. Sprinkle topping over batter. Bake at 400°F for 28 to 33 minutes for 8-inch pan (or 20 to 25 minutes for 9-inch pan) or until golden. Serve warm. *Makes 9 servings*

## Lemon Cranberry Loaves

1¼ cups finely chopped fresh cranberries
½ cup finely chopped walnuts
¼ cup granulated sugar
1 package DUNCAN HINES® Moist Deluxe® Lemon Supreme Cake Mix
¾ cup milk
1 package (3 ounces) cream cheese, softened
4 eggs
Confectioners' sugar

**1.** Preheat oven to 350°F. Grease and flour two 8½×4½-inch loaf pans.

**2.** Stir together cranberries, walnuts and granulated sugar in large bowl; set aside.

**3.** Combine cake mix, milk and cream cheese in large bowl. Beat at medium speed with electric mixer for 2 minutes. Add eggs, 1 at a time, beating for 2 minutes. Fold in cranberry mixture. Pour into prepared pans. Bake at 350°F for 45 to 50 minutes or until toothpick inserted in centers comes out clean. Cool in pans 15 minutes. Loosen loaves from pans. Invert onto cooling rack. Turn right side up. Cool completely. Dust with confectioners' sugar. *Makes 24 slices*

**Hint:** To quickly chop cranberries or walnuts, use a food processor fitted with a steel blade and pulse until evenly chopped.

## Banana Coffeecake

*Streusel*
- ½ cup chopped pecans
- ⅓ cup firmly packed brown sugar
- 1 teaspoon ground cinnamon
- 1 teaspoon ground nutmeg

*Cake*
- 1 package DUNCAN HINES® Moist Deluxe® Banana Supreme Cake Mix
- 1 package (4-serving size) vanilla-flavor instant pudding and pie filling mix
- 4 eggs
- 1 cup ripe mashed bananas
- ⅓ cup vegetable oil
- ¼ cup water
- Confectioners' sugar

**1.** Preheat oven to 350°F. Grease and flour 10-inch Bundt pan or tube pan.

**2.** For streusel, combine pecans, brown sugar, cinnamon and nutmeg in small bowl. Stir until blended. Set aside.

**3.** For cake, combine cake mix, pudding mix, eggs, bananas, oil and water in large bowl. Beat at medium speed with electric mixer for 2 minutes. Pour half of batter into prepared pan. Sprinkle streusel over batter. Spread remaining batter over streusel. Swirl with knife in figure-eight pattern. Bake at 350°F for 55 to 60 minutes or until toothpick inserted in center comes out clean. Cool in pan 25 minutes. Invert onto cooling rack. Cool completely. Dust with confectioners' sugar.

*Makes 12 to 16 servings*

**Note:** Coffeecake can be made using two greased and floured 8½×4½-inch loaf pans. Pour batter into prepared pans. Sprinkle streusel on top and press mixture lightly with fork. Bake at 350°F for 45 to 50 minutes or until toothpick inserted in center comes out clean.

**Hint:** A quick confectioners' sugar glaze can be used to dress up any coffeecake or quick bread and give it a professional look. Be sure to wait until the bread has cooled slightly before adding the glaze, or it will be absorbed into the bread.

## Orange Zucchini Loaves

*Loaves*

    1 package DUNCAN HINES® Moist Deluxe® Orange Supreme Cake Mix
    3 egg whites
    ¾ cup water
    ⅓ cup vegetable oil
    1 teaspoon ground cinnamon
    1 cup grated zucchini
    2 teaspoons grated orange peel

*Syrup*

    ¼ cup granulated sugar
    2 tablespoons orange juice
    Confectioners' sugar, for garnish
    Orange slices for garnish (optional)

**1.** Preheat oven to 350°F. Grease and flour two 8½×4½×2½-inch loaf pans.

**2.** For loaves, combine cake mix, egg whites, water, oil and cinnamon in large bowl. Beat at low speed with electric mixer until moistened. Beat at medium speed for 2 minutes. Fold in zucchini and orange peel. Divide evenly in prepared pans. Bake at 350°F for 50 to 55 minutes or until toothpick inserted in center comes out clean. Cool in pans 15 minutes. Loosen loaves from pans. Invert onto cooling racks. Turn right side up. Poke holes in tops of warm loaves with toothpick or long-tined fork.

**3.** For syrup, combine granulated sugar and orange juice in small saucepan. Cook on medium heat, stirring constantly, until sugar dissolves. Spoon hot syrup evenly over each loaf. Cool completely. Garnish with confectioners' sugar and orange slices, if desired.

*Makes 2 loaves (24 slices)*

**Note:** This recipe contains no cholesterol.

# Easy-to-Make Cakes

1 package DUNCAN HINES® Angel Food Cake Mix
2¼ teaspoons ground cinnamon, divided
1½ cups frozen whipped topping, thawed

**1.** Preheat oven to 350°F.

**2.** Prepare cake following package directions. Spoon one-third of batter into ungreased 10-inch tube pan. Spread evenly. Sprinkle 1 teaspoon cinnamon over batter with small fine sieve. Repeat. Top with remaining cake batter. Bake and cool following package directions.

**3.** Combine whipped topping and ¼ teaspoon cinnamon in small bowl. Serve with cake slices.                                   *Makes 12 to 16 servings*

**Hint:** To slice cake, use a serrated knife and cut in a sawing motion.

## Chocolate Chip Cookie Cake

1 package DUNCAN HINES® Moist Deluxe® Yellow Cake Mix
1 package (4-serving size) vanilla-flavor instant pudding and pie filling mix
4 eggs
1 cup water
⅓ cup vegetable oil
1 package (12 ounces) semisweet chocolate chips
1½ cups finely chopped pecans
Confectioners' sugar for garnish

**1.** Preheat oven to 350°F. Grease and flour 10-inch Bundt pan.

**2.** Combine cake mix, pudding mix, eggs, water and oil in large mixing bowl. Beat at medium speed with electric mixer for 2 minutes. Stir in chocolate chips and pecans. Pour into prepared pan. Bake at 350°F for 50 to 60 minutes or until toothpick inserted in center comes out clean. Cool in pan 25 minutes. Invert onto serving plate. Cool completely. Dust with confectioners' sugar, if desired.

*Makes 12 to 16 servings*

## Orange Soak Cake

*Cake*
1 package DUNCAN HINES® Moist Deluxe® Orange Supreme Cake Mix

*Glaze*
2 cups confectioners' sugar
⅓ cup orange juice
2 tablespoons butter or margarine, melted
1 tablespoon water

**1.** Preheat oven to 350°F. Grease and flour 13×9×2-inch pan.

**2.** For cake, prepare and bake following package directions for basic recipe. Poke holes in top of warm cake with tines of fork or toothpick.

**3.** For glaze, combine confectioners' sugar, orange juice, melted butter and water in medium bowl. Pour slowly over top of cake allowing glaze to soak into warm cake. Cool completely.

*Makes 12 to 16 servings*

**Hint:** Sift confectioners' sugar before preparing glaze.

## Upside-Down German Chocolate Cake

1½ cups flaked coconut
1½ cups chopped pecans
   1 package DUNCAN HINES® Moist Deluxe® German Chocolate or
      Classic Chocolate Cake Mix
   1 package (8 ounces) cream cheese, softened
½ cup butter or margarine, melted
   1 pound (3½ to 4 cups) confectioners' sugar

**1.** Preheat oven to 350°F. Grease and flour 13×9-inch pan.

**2.** Spread coconut evenly on bottom of prepared pan. Sprinkle with pecans. Prepare cake mix as directed on package. Pour over coconut and pecans. Combine cream cheese and melted butter in medium mixing bowl. Beat at low speed with electric mixer until creamy. Add confectioners' sugar; beat until blended and smooth. Drop by spoonfuls evenly over cake batter. Bake at 350°F for 45 to 50 minutes or until toothpick inserted halfway to bottom of cake comes out clean. Cool completely in pan. To serve, cut into individual pieces; turn upside down onto plate.

*Makes 12 to 16 servings*

### Tip

Flaked and shredded sweetened coconut is readily available year-round in plastic bags and cans. Store leftover flaked or shredded coconut in an airtight container for up to 4 weeks in the refrigerator or up to 6 months in the freezer.

**Upside-Down German Chocolate Cake**

## Sock-It-To-Me Cake

*Streusel Filling*

   1 package DUNCAN HINES® Moist Deluxe® Butter Recipe Golden Cake
      Mix, divided
   2 tablespoons brown sugar
   2 teaspoons ground cinnamon
   1 cup finely chopped pecans

*Cake*

   4 eggs
   1 cup dairy sour cream
   $\frac{1}{3}$ cup vegetable oil
   $\frac{1}{4}$ cup water
   $\frac{1}{4}$ cup granulated sugar

*Glaze*

   1 cup confectioners' sugar
   1 or 2 tablespoons milk

**1.** Preheat oven to 375°F. Grease and flour 10-inch tube pan.

**2.** For streusel filling, combine 2 tablespoons cake mix, brown sugar and cinnamon in medium bowl. Stir in pecans. Set aside.

**3.** For cake, combine remaining cake mix, eggs, sour cream, oil, water and granulated sugar in large bowl. Beat at medium speed with electric mixer 2 minutes. Pour two-thirds of batter into prepared pan. Sprinkle with streusel filling. Spoon remaining batter evenly over filling. Bake at 375°F for 45 to 55 minutes or until toothpick inserted in center comes out clean. Cool in pan 25 minutes. Invert onto serving plate. Cool completely.

**4.** For glaze, combine confectioners' sugar and milk in small bowl. Stir until smooth. Drizzle over cake.                  ***Makes 12 to 16 servings***

**Hint:** For a quick glaze, place $\frac{1}{2}$ cup Duncan Hines® Creamy Home-Style Vanilla Frosting in small microwave-safe bowl. Microwave at **HIGH** (100% power) 10 seconds; add 5 to 10 seconds, if needed. Stir until smooth and thin.

## Dump Cake

**1 can (20 ounces) crushed pineapple with juice, undrained**
**1 can (21 ounces) cherry pie filling**
**1 package DUNCAN HINES® Moist Deluxe® Yellow Cake Mix**
**1 cup chopped pecans or walnuts**
**½ cup butter or margarine, cut into thin slices**

**1.** Preheat oven to 350°F. Grease 13×9-inch pan.

**2.** Dump pineapple with juice into prepared pan. Spread evenly. Dump in pie filling. Spread evenly. Sprinkle cake mix evenly over cherry layer. Sprinkle pecans over cake mix. Dot with butter. Bake at 350°F for 50 minutes or until top is lightly browned. Serve warm or at room temperature. ***Makes 12 to 16 servings***

**Hint:** You can use Duncan Hines® Moist Deluxe® Pineapple Supreme Cake Mix in place of Moist Deluxe® Yellow Cake Mix.

## Hot Fudge Pudding Cake

**1 package DUNCAN HINES® Moist Deluxe® Devil's Food Cake Mix**
**2 eggs**
**1 cup water**
**1 cup chopped pecans**
**½ cup granulated sugar**
**½ cup packed brown sugar**
**2 tablespoons unsweetened cocoa powder**
**1 cup boiling water**
**Whipped topping for garnish**

**1.** Preheat oven to 350°F. Grease and flour 13×9-inch pan.

**2.** Combine cake mix, eggs and water in large mixing bowl. Beat at medium speed with electric mixer for 2 minutes. Stir in pecans. Pour into prepared pan.

**3.** Combine granulated sugar, brown sugar and cocoa in small bowl. Sprinkle over batter. Pour boiling water over all. *Do not stir.* Bake at 350°F for 45 minutes or until toothpick inserted in center halfway to bottom comes out clean. Serve warm with whipped topping. ***Makes 12 to 16 servings***

**Hint:** For a richer dessert, use Duncan Hines® Moist Deluxe® Dark Chocolate Cake Mix in place of Devil's Food Cake Mix.

Dump Cake

## Take-Along Cake

1 package DUNCAN HINES® Moist Deluxe® Swiss Chocolate Cake Mix
1 package (12 ounces) semisweet chocolate chips
1 cup miniature marshmallows
¼ cup butter or margarine, melted
½ cup packed brown sugar
½ cup chopped pecans or walnuts

1. Preheat oven to 350°F. Grease and flour 13×9-inch pan.

2. Prepare cake mix as directed on package. Add chocolate chips and marshmallows to batter. Pour into prepared pan. Drizzle melted butter over batter. Sprinkle with sugar and top with pecans. Bake at 350°F for 45 to 55 minutes or until toothpick inserted in center comes out clean. Serve warm or cool completely in pan.

*Makes 12 to 16 servings*

**Hint:** To keep leftover pecans fresh, store them in the freezer in an airtight container.

## Coconut Pound Cake

1 package DUNCAN HINES® Moist Deluxe® French Vanilla Cake Mix
1 package (4-serving size) coconut cream-flavor instant pudding and pie filling mix
4 eggs
1 cup water
⅓ cup vegetable oil
1 cup flaked coconut
1 cup confectioners' sugar
2 tablespoons milk
Additional coconut for garnish (optional)

1. Preheat oven to 350°F. Grease and flour 10-inch Bundt pan.

2. Combine cake mix, pudding mix, eggs, water and oil in large mixing bowl. Beat at medium speed with electric mixer for 2 minutes. Fold in 1 cup coconut. Pour into prepared pan. Bake at 350°F for 45 to 50 minutes or until toothpick inserted in center comes out clean. Cool in pan 25 minutes. Invert onto serving plate. Mix sugar and milk in small bowl until smooth. Drizzle over cake. Sprinkle with additional coconut, if desired.

*Makes 12 to 16 servings*

**Hint:** Garnish the top of the cake with toasted coconut. To toast coconut, spread on baking sheet and bake at 350°F for 3 minutes. Stir and bake 1 to 2 minutes longer or until light golden brown.

## Pineapple Upside-Down Cake

*Topping*
- ½ cup butter or margarine
- 1 cup firmly packed brown sugar
- 1 can (20 ounces) pineapple slices, well drained
- Maraschino cherries, halved and drained
- Walnut halves

*Cake*
- 1 package DUNCAN HINES® Moist Deluxe® Pineapple Supreme Cake Mix
- 1 package (4-serving size) vanilla-flavor instant pudding and pie filling mix
- 4 eggs
- 1 cup water
- ½ cup oil

**1.** Preheat oven to 350°F.

**2.** For topping, melt butter over low heat in 12-inch cast-iron skillet or skillet with oven-proof handle. Remove from heat. Stir in brown sugar. Spread to cover bottom of skillet. Arrange pineapple slices, maraschino cherries and walnut halves in skillet. Set aside.

**3.** For cake, combine cake mix, pudding mix, eggs, water and oil in large mixing bowl. Beat at medium speed with electric mixer for 2 minutes. Pour batter evenly over fruit in skillet. Bake at 350°F for 1 hour or until toothpick inserted in center comes out clean. Invert onto serving plate. ***Makes 16 to 20 servings***

**Note:** Cake can be made in a 13×9×2-inch pan. Bake at 350°F for 45 to 55 minutes or until toothpick inserted in center comes out clean. Cake is also delicious using Duncan Hines® Moist Deluxe® Yellow Cake Mix.

## Strawberry Stripe Refrigerator Cake

*Cake*

1 package DUNCAN HINES® Moist Deluxe® Classic White Cake Mix

2 packages (10 ounces each) frozen sweetened strawberry slices, thawed

*Topping*

1 package (4-serving size) vanilla-flavor instant pudding and pie filling mix

1 cup milk

1 cup whipping cream, whipped

Fresh strawberries for garnish (optional)

**1.** Preheat oven to 350°F. Grease and flour 13×9×2-inch pan.

**2.** For cake, prepare, bake and cool following package directions. Poke holes 1 inch apart in top of cake using handle of wooden spoon. Puree thawed strawberries with juice in blender or food processor. Spoon evenly over top of cake, allowing mixture to soak into holes.

**3.** For topping, combine pudding mix and milk in large bowl. Stir until smooth. Fold in whipped cream. Spread over cake. Decorate with fresh strawberries, if desired. Refrigerate at least 4 hours. *Makes 12 to 16 servings*

**Variation:** For a Neapolitan Refrigerator Cake, replace the White Cake Mix with Duncan Hines® Moist Deluxe® Devil's Food Cake Mix and follow directions listed above.

## Orange Glazed Pound Cake

1 package DUNCAN HINES® Moist Deluxe® Butter Recipe Golden Cake
    Mix
4 eggs
1 cup sour cream
⅓ cup vegetable oil
¼ cup plus 1 to 2 tablespoons orange juice, divided
2 tablespoons grated orange peel
1 cup confectioners' sugar

**1.** Preheat oven to 375°F. Grease and flour 10-inch Bundt pan.

**2.** Combine cake mix, eggs, sour cream, oil, ¼ cup orange juice and orange peel in large bowl. Beat at medium speed with electric mixer for 2 minutes. Pour into prepared pan. Bake at 375°F for 45 to 50 minutes or until toothpick inserted in center comes out clean. Cool in pan 25 minutes. Invert onto cooling rack. Cool completely.

**3.** Combine sugar and remaining 1 to 2 tablespoons orange juice in small bowl; stir until smooth. Drizzle over cake. Garnish as desired.     *Makes 12 to 16 servings*

### Tip

When grating orange peel, grate only the outer orange layer of the skin, which is very sweet and flavorful. Avoid grating into the white pith, as it is has a bitter taste.

## Banana-Coconut Crunch Cake

*Cake*

   1 package DUNCAN HINES® Moist Deluxe® Banana Supreme Cake Mix
   1 package (4-serving size) banana-flavor instant pudding and pie
      filling mix
   1 can (16 ounces) fruit cocktail, in juices, undrained
   4 eggs
   ¼ cup vegetable oil
   1 cup flaked coconut
   ½ cup chopped pecans
   ½ cup firmly packed brown sugar

*Glaze*

   ¾ cup granulated sugar
   ½ cup butter or margarine
   ½ cup evaporated milk
   1⅓ cups flaked coconut

**1.** Preheat oven to 350°F. Grease and flour 13×9×2-inch pan.

**2.** For cake, combine cake mix, pudding mix, fruit cocktail with juice, eggs and oil in large bowl. Beat at medium speed with electric mixer for 4 minutes. Stir in 1 cup coconut. Pour into prepared pan. Combine pecans and brown sugar in small bowl. Stir until well mixed. Sprinkle over batter. Bake at 350°F for 45 to 50 minutes or until toothpick inserted in center comes out clean.

**3.** For glaze, combine granulated sugar, butter and evaporated milk in medium saucepan. Bring to a boil. Cook for 2 minutes, stirring occasionally. Remove from heat. Stir in 1⅓ cups coconut. Pour over warm cake. Serve warm or at room temperature.                              ***Makes 12 to 16 servings***

**Hint:** Assemble all ingredients and utensils together before beginning the recipe.

## Chocolate Streusel Cake

*Streusel*

    1 package DUNCAN HINES® Moist Deluxe® Devil's Food Cake Mix, divided

    1 cup finely chopped pecans

    2 tablespoons brown sugar

    2 teaspoons ground cinnamon

*Cake*

    3 eggs

    $1\frac{1}{3}$ cups water

    $\frac{1}{2}$ cup vegetable oil

*Topping*

    1 container (8 ounces) frozen whipped topping, thawed

    3 tablespoons sifted unsweetened cocoa powder

    Chopped pecans for garnish (optional)

    Chocolate curls for garnish (optional)

**1.** Preheat oven to 350°F. Grease and flour 10-inch Bundt pan.

**2.** For streusel, combine 2 tablespoons cake mix, 1 cup pecans, brown sugar and cinnamon. Set aside.

**3.** For cake, combine remaining cake mix, eggs, water and oil in large bowl. Beat at medium speed with electric mixer for 2 minutes. Pour two-thirds of batter into prepared pan. Sprinkle with reserved streusel. Pour remaining batter evenly over streusel. Bake at 350°F for 55 to 60 minutes or until toothpick inserted in center comes out clean. Cool in pan 25 minutes. Invert onto serving plate. Cool completely.

**4.** For topping, place whipped topping in medium bowl. Fold in cocoa until blended. Spread on cooled cake. Garnish with chopped pecans and chocolate curls, if desired. Refrigerate until ready to serve.

*Makes 12 to 16 servings*

**Note:** For chocolate curls, warm chocolate in microwave oven at HIGH (100% power) for 5 to 10 seconds. Make chocolate curls by holding a sharp vegetable peeler against the flat side of a chocolate block and bringing the blade toward you. Apply firm pressure for thicker, more open curls or light pressure for tighter curls.

## Fantasy Angel Food Cake

**1 package DUNCAN HINES® Angel Food Cake Mix**
**Red and green food coloring**
**1 container DUNCAN HINES® Creamy Home-Style Cream Cheese**
**Frosting**

**1.** Preheat oven to 350°F.

**2.** Prepare cake following package directions. Divide batter into thirds and place in 3 different bowls. Add a few drops red food coloring to one. Add a few drops green food coloring to another. Stir each until well blended. Leave the third one plain. Spoon pink batter into ungreased 10-inch tube pan. Cover with white batter and top with green batter. Bake and cool following package directions.

**3.** To make cream cheese glaze, heat frosting in microwave at **HIGH** (100% power) 20 to 30 seconds. Do not overheat. Stir until smooth. Set aside $^1/_4$ cup warm glaze. Spoon remaining glaze on top and sides of cake to completely cover. Divide remaining glaze in half and place in 2 different bowls. Add a few drops red food coloring to one. Add a few drops green food coloring to the other. Stir each until well blended. Using a teaspoon, drizzle green glaze around edge of cake so it will run down sides. Repeat with pink glaze.                    *Makes 16 servings*

**Hint:** For marble cake, drop batter by spoonfuls, alternating colors frequently.

## Lemon Crumb Cake

1 package DUNCAN HINES® Moist Deluxe® Lemon Supreme Cake Mix
3 eggs
1⅓ cups water
⅓ cup vegetable oil
1 cup all-purpose flour
½ cup packed light brown sugar
½ teaspoon baking powder
½ cup butter or margarine

1. Preheat oven to 350°F. Grease and flour 13×9-inch pan.

2. Combine cake mix, eggs, water and oil in large mixing bowl. Beat at medium speed with electric mixer for 2 minutes. Pour into prepared pan. Combine flour, sugar and baking powder in small bowl. Cut in butter until crumbly. Sprinkle evenly over batter. Bake at 350°F for 35 to 40 minutes or until toothpick inserted in center comes out clean. Cool completely in pan. *Makes 12 to 16 servings*

**Hint:** Butter or margarine will cut more easily into the flour mixture if it is chilled. Use two knives or a pastry cutter to cut the mixture into crumbs.

## Applesauce Walnut Cake

1 package DUNCAN HINES® Moist Deluxe® Butter Recipe Golden Cake Mix
3 eggs
1⅓ cups applesauce
½ cup butter or margarine, melted
1 teaspoon ground cinnamon
½ cup chopped walnuts
Confectioners' sugar for garnish

1. Preheat oven to 375°F. Grease and flour 10-inch Bundt or tube pan.

2. Combine cake mix, eggs, applesauce, melted butter and cinnamon in large bowl. Beat at low speed with electric mixer until moistened. Beat at medium speed for 4 minutes. Stir in walnuts. Pour into prepared pan. Bake at 375°F for 45 to 55 minutes or until toothpick inserted in center comes out clean. Cool in pan 25 minutes. Invert cake onto serving plate. Cool completely. Dust with confectioners' sugar. *Makes 12 to 16 servings*

**Hint:** This cake is also delicious using chopped pecans instead of walnuts.

## Strawberry Pound Cake

1 package DUNCAN HINES® Moist Deluxe® Strawberry Supreme Cake
Mix
1 package (4-serving size) vanilla-flavor instant pudding and pie filling
mix
4 eggs
1 cup water
$\frac{1}{3}$ cup vegetable oil
1 cup mini semisweet chocolate chips
$\frac{2}{3}$ cup DUNCAN HINES® Creamy Home-Style Chocolate Buttercream
Frosting

**1.** Preheat oven to 350°F. Grease and flour 10-inch Bundt pan.

**2.** Combine cake mix, pudding mix, eggs, water and oil in large mixing bowl. Beat at low speed with electric mixer until moistened. Beat at medium speed for 2 minutes. Stir in chocolate chips. Pour into prepared pan. Bake at 350°F for 55 to 60 minutes or until toothpick inserted in center comes out clean. Cool in pan 25 minutes. Invert onto cooling rack. Cool completely.

**3.** Place frosting in 1-cup glass measuring cup. Microwave at HIGH for 10 to 15 seconds. Stir until smooth. Drizzle over top of cooled cake.

*Makes 12 to 16 servings*

**Hint:** Store leftover Chocolate Buttercream frosting, covered, in the refrigerator. Spread the frosting between graham crackers for a quick snack.

### Tip

Once cake batter is mixed and poured into the prepared pan, immediately place the pan in the preheated oven. Cake batter should not sit before baking because the chemical leaveners will begin working as soon as they are mixed with liquids.

# Festive Layer Cakes

## Refreshing Lemon Cake

1 package DUNCAN HINES® Moist Deluxe® Butter Recipe Golden
   Cake Mix
1 container DUNCAN HINES® Creamy Home-Style Cream Cheese
   Frosting
¾ cup purchased lemon curd
   Lemon drop candies, crushed for garnish (optional)

**1.** Preheat oven to 375°F. Grease and flour two 8- or 9-inch round cake pans.

**2.** Prepare, bake and cool cake following package directions for basic recipe.

**3.** To assemble, place one cake layer on serving plate. Place ¼ cup Cream Cheese frosting in small resealable plastic bag. Snip off one corner. Pipe a bead of frosting on top of layer around outer edge. Fill remaining area with lemon curd. Top with second cake layer. Spread remaining frosting on sides and top of cake. Garnish top of cake with crushed lemon candies, if desired.

*Makes 12 to 16 servings*

**Hint:** You can substitute Duncan Hines® Vanilla or Buttercream Frosting for the Cream Cheese frosting, if desired.

## Easy Cream Cake

1 package DUNCAN HINES® Moist Deluxe® Classic White Cake Mix
3 egg whites
1⅓ cups half-and-half
2 tablespoons vegetable oil
1 cup flaked coconut, finely chopped
½ cup finely chopped pecans
2 containers DUNCAN HINES® Creamy Home-Style Cream Cheese Frosting

**1.** Preheat oven to 350°F. Grease and flour three 8-inch round cake pans.

**2.** Combine cake mix, egg whites, half-and-half, oil, coconut and pecans in large bowl. Beat at low speed with electric mixer until moistened. Beat at medium speed 2 minutes. Pour into prepared pans. Bake at 350°F for 22 to 25 minutes or until toothpick inserted in center comes out clean. Cool following package directions.

**3.** To assemble, place one cake layer on serving plate. Spread with ¾ cup Cream Cheese frosting. Place second cake layer on top. Spread with ¾ cup frosting. Top with third layer. Spread ¾ cup frosting on top only. Garnish top as desired.

*Makes 12 to 16 servings*

**Hint:** Spread leftover frosting between graham crackers for an easy snack.

### Tip

If cake layers cool too long in the baking pans, they can become difficult to remove. If this happens, simply place the pans in a preheated 350°F oven for 3 to 5 minutes, then turn the cake layers out onto wire racks.

Easy Cream Cake

## Banana Fudge Layer Cake

    **1 package DUNCAN HINES® Moist Deluxe® Yellow Cake Mix**
**1⅓ cups water**
  **3 eggs**
  **⅓ cup vegetable oil**
  **1 cup mashed ripe bananas (about 3 medium)**
  **1 container DUNCAN HINES® Chocolate Frosting**

**1.** Preheat oven to 350°F. Grease and flour two 9-inch round cake pans.

**2.** Combine cake mix, water, eggs and oil in large bowl. Beat at low speed with electric mixer until moistened. Beat at medium speed 2 minutes. Stir in bananas.

**3.** Pour into prepared pans. Bake at 350°F for 28 to 31 minutes or until toothpick inserted in center comes out clean. Cool in pans 15 minutes. Remove from pans; cool completely.

**4.** Fill and frost cake with frosting. Garnish as desired.     ***Makes 12 to 16 servings***

## Strawberry Raspberry Cake

    **1 package DUNCAN HINES® Moist Deluxe® Strawberry Supreme Cake Mix**
  **2 ounces white chocolate baking bar, grated, divided**
**½ cup red raspberry jam**
  **1 container DUNCAN HINES® Creamy Home-Style Classic Vanilla Frosting**
  **Red raspberries (optional)**

**1.** Preheat oven to 350°F. Grease and flour two 9-inch round cake pans.

**2.** Prepare cake mix as directed on package. Stir in ½ cup grated chocolate. Set aside remaining chocolate for garnish. Pour batter into prepared pans. Bake at 350°F for 28 to 31 minutes or until toothpick inserted in center comes out clean. Cool in pans 15 minutes. Invert onto cooling racks. Cool completely.

**3.** Place one cake layer on serving plate. Spread with jam. Top with second cake layer. Frost sides and top of cake with frosting. Garnish with remaining grated chocolate and raspberries.     ***Makes 12 to 16 servings***

## Delicate White Chocolate Cake

1 package DUNCAN HINES® Moist Deluxe® White Cake Mix
1 package (4-serving size) vanilla-flavor instant pudding and pie filling mix
4 egg whites
1 cup water
½ cup vegetable oil
5 ounces finely chopped white chocolate
1 cup cherry preserves
8 drops red food coloring (optional)
2 cups whipping cream, chilled
2 tablespoons confectioners' sugar
Maraschino cherries for garnish
1 ounce white chocolate shavings for garnish

**1.** Preheat oven to 350°F. Cut waxed paper circles to fit bottoms of three 9-inch round cake pans. Grease bottoms and sides of pans. Line with waxed paper circles.

**2.** Combine cake mix, pudding mix, egg whites, water and oil in large mixing bowl. Beat at medium speed with electric mixer for 2 minutes. Fold in chopped white chocolate. Pour into prepared pans. Bake at 350°F for 18 to 22 minutes or until toothpick inserted in center comes out clean. Cool in pans 15 minutes. Invert onto cooling racks. Peel off waxed paper. Cool completely.

**3.** Combine cherry preserves and food coloring, if desired. Stir to blend color.

**4.** Beat whipping cream in large bowl until soft peaks form. Add sugar gradually. Beat until stiff peaks form.

**5.** To assemble, place one cake layer on serving plate. Spread ½ cup cherry preserves over cake. Place second cake layer on top. Spread with remaining preserves. Place third cake layer on top. Frost sides and top of cake with whipped cream. Decorate with maraschino cherries and white chocolate shavings. Refrigerate until ready to serve.

*Makes 12 to 16 servings*

## Chocolate Toffee Cream Cake

1 package DUNCAN HINES® Moist Deluxe® Dark Chocolate Fudge Cake
    Mix
3 eggs
1⅓ cups water
½ cup vegetable oil
1 package (6 ounces) milk chocolate English toffee bits, divided
1 container (12 ounces) extra creamy non-dairy whipped topping,
    thawed

**1.** Preheat oven to 350°F. Grease and flour two 9-inch round cake pans.

**2.** Blend cake mix, eggs, water and oil in large mixing bowl until moistened. Beat at medium speed with electric mixer for 4 minutes. Pour into prepared pans. Bake at 350°F for 30 to 33 minutes or until toothpick inserted in center comes out clean. Cool in pans 15 minutes. Remove from pans. Cool completely.

**3.** Reserve ¼ cup toffee bits; fold remaining bits into whipped topping. Place one cake layer on serving plate; spread with ¾ cup topping mixture. Top with remaining layer. Frost sides and top with remaining topping mixture; garnish with reserved bits. Refrigerate until ready to serve.         *Makes 12 to 16 servings*

**Hint:** If chocolate toffee bits are not available, 4 chocolate covered toffee candy bars can be substituted. Chop bars in a food processor until small pieces form.

Chocolate Toffee Cream Cake

## Double Berry Layer Cake

1 package DUNCAN HINES® Moist Deluxe® Strawberry Supreme Cake
  Mix
$^2/_3$ cup strawberry jam, divided
$2^1/_2$ cups fresh blueberries, rinsed, drained and divided
1 container (8 ounces) frozen whipped topping, thawed and divided
  Fresh strawberry slices for garnish

**1.** Preheat oven to 350°F. Grease and flour two 9-inch round cake pans.

**2.** Prepare, bake and cool cake following package directions for basic recipe.

**3.** Place one cake layer on serving plate. Spread with $^1/_3$ cup strawberry jam. Arrange 1 cup blueberries on jam. Spread half the whipped topping to within $^1/_2$ inch of cake edge. Place second cake layer on top. Repeat with remaining $^1/_3$ cup strawberry jam, 1 cup blueberries and remaining whipped topping. Garnish with strawberry slices and remaining $^1/_2$ cup blueberries. Refrigerate until ready to serve.

*Makes 12 servings*

**Hint:** For best results, cut cake with serrated knife; clean knife after each slice.

## Chocolate Peanut Butter Frosted Cake

1 package DUNCAN HINES® Moist Deluxe® Devil's Food Cake Mix
$1^1/_3$ cups water
$^1/_2$ cup vegetable oil
3 eggs
1 container DUNCAN HINES® Chocolate Frosting
$^1/_2$ cup creamy peanut butter
$^1/_2$ cup chopped peanuts

**1.** Preheat oven to 350°F. Grease and lightly flour two 9-inch round cake pans.

**2.** Combine cake mix, water, oil and eggs in large mixing bowl. Beat at low speed with electric mixer until moistened. Beat at medium speed for 2 minutes. Pour into prepared pans. Bake at 350°F for 30 to 33 minutes or until toothpick inserted in center comes out clean. Cool in pans 15 minutes; remove from pans. Cool completely.

**3.** Mix frosting and peanut butter in small bowl until smooth. Fill and frost cake. Sprinkle with peanuts.

*Makes 12 to 16 servings*

## Carrot Layer Cake

*Cake*

    1 package DUNCAN HINES® Moist Deluxe® Classic Yellow Cake Mix
    4 eggs
    ½ cup vegetable oil
    3 cups grated carrots
    1 cup finely chopped nuts
    2 teaspoons ground cinnamon

*Cream Cheese Frosting*

    1 package (8 ounces) cream cheese, softened
    ¼ cup butter or margarine, softened
    2 teaspoons vanilla extract
    4 cups confectioners' sugar

**1.** Preheat oven to 350°F. Grease and flour two 8- or 9-inch round baking pans.

**2.** For cake, combine cake mix, eggs, oil, carrots, nuts and cinnamon in large bowl. Beat at low speed with electric mixer until moistened. Beat at medium speed for 2 minutes. Pour into prepared pans. Bake at 350°F for 35 to 40 minutes or until toothpick inserted in centers comes out clean. Cool.

**3.** For cream cheese frosting, place cream cheese, butter and vanilla extract in large bowl. Beat at low speed until smooth and creamy. Add confectioners' sugar gradually, beating until smooth. Add more sugar to thicken, or milk or water to thin frosting, as needed. Fill and frost cooled cake. Garnish with whole pecans.

*Makes 12 to 16 servings*

Carrot Layer Cake

## Ribbon Cake

*Cake*

1 package DUNCAN HINES® Moist Deluxe® Classic White Cake Mix
¼ cup flaked coconut, chopped
¼ cup natural pistachio nuts, finely chopped
Green food coloring
¼ cup maraschino cherries, drained, finely chopped
Red food coloring

*Filling and Frosting*

3¼ cups confectioners' sugar
½ cup shortening
⅓ cup water
¼ cup powdered non-dairy creamer
1½ teaspoons vanilla extract
¼ teaspoon salt
Green food coloring
½ cup natural pistachio nuts, finely chopped
¾ cup cherry jam
Whole maraschino cherries with stems for garnish
Mint leaves for garnish

**1.** Preheat oven to 350°F. Grease and flour three 8-inch square baking pans.

**2.** For cake, prepare cake mix following package directions for basic recipe. Combine 1¾ cups batter and coconut in small bowl; set aside. Combine 1¾ cups batter, pistachio nuts and 5 drops green food coloring in small bowl; set aside. Combine remaining batter, ¼ cup chopped maraschino cherries and 2 drops red food coloring. Pour batters into separate pans. Bake at 350°F for 18 minutes or until toothpick inserted in center comes out clean. Cool following package directions. Trim edges of cake.

**3.** For filling and frosting, combine confectioners' sugar, shortening, water, non-dairy creamer, vanilla extract, salt and 5 drops green food coloring in large bowl. Beat for 3 minutes at medium speed with electric mixer. Beat for 5 minutes at high speed. Add more confectioners' sugar to thicken or water to thin as needed. Add remaining ½ cup pistachio nuts. Stir until blended.

**4.** To assemble, spread green and white cake layers with cherry jam. Stack layers. Top with pink layer. Frost sides and top of cake. Garnish with whole maraschino cherries and mint leaves. ***Makes 12 to 16 servings***

**Hint:** To save time, use Duncan Hines® Creamy Home-Style Vanilla Frosting. Tint with several drops green food coloring.

## Autumn Gold Pumpkin Cake

1 package DUNCAN HINES® Moist Deluxe® Butter Recipe Golden Cake
   Mix
3 eggs
1 cup water
1 cup solid pack pumpkin
1½ teaspoons ground cinnamon, divided
¼ teaspoon ground ginger
¼ teaspoon ground nutmeg
1 cup chopped walnuts
1 container DUNCAN HINES® Vanilla Frosting
¼ cup coarsely chopped walnuts for garnish

**1.** Preheat oven to 375°F. Grease and flour two 8-inch round cake pans. Combine cake mix, eggs, water, pumpkin, 1 teaspoon cinnamon, ginger and nutmeg in large mixing bowl. Beat at medium speed with electric mixer for 4 minutes.

**2.** Stir in 1 cup walnuts. Pour into prepared pans. Bake at 375°F for 30 to 35 minutes or until toothpick inserted in center comes out clean. Cool in pans 15 minutes. Remove from pans. Cool completely.

**3.** Combine frosting and remaining ½ teaspoon cinnamon. Stir until blended. Fill and frost cake. Garnish with ¼ cup walnuts.    *Makes 12 to 16 servings*

## Chocolate Angel Food Dessert

1 package DUNCAN HINES® Angel Food Cake Mix
16 large marshmallows
½ cup milk
1 package (11 ounces) milk chocolate chips
1 pint whipping cream
¼ cup semisweet chocolate chips
1½ teaspoons shortening

**1.** Preheat oven to 375°F. Prepare, bake and cool cake following package directions.

**2.** Melt marshmallows and milk in heavy saucepan over low heat. Remove from heat; stir in milk chocolate chips until melted. Cool to room temperature. Beat whipping cream in large bowl until stiff peaks form. Fold cooled chocolate mixture into whipped cream. Refrigerate until of spreading consistency.

**3.** To assemble, split cake horizontally into 3 even layers. Place 1 cake layer on serving plate. Spread with one-fourth of frosting. Repeat with second layer. Top with third layer. Frost side and top with remaining frosting. Refrigerate.

**4.** For drizzle, place semisweet chocolate chips and shortening in 1-cup glass measuring cup. Microwave at MEDIUM (50% power) for 1 minute. Stir until smooth. Drizzle melted chocolate around outer top edge of cake, allowing mixture to run down side unevenly. Refrigerate until ready to serve.     *Makes 12 to 16 servings*

### Tip

To evenly cut a cake horizontally in half, remove the cake from the pan and place it on a flat surface. Measure the cake with a ruler and mark a cutting line with toothpicks. Cut through the cake with a long serrated knife, just above the toothpicks. For the best results, use a sawing motion while cutting.

## Cookies & Creme Cake

   1 package DUNCAN HINES® Moist Deluxe® White Cake Mix
   3 egg whites
1⅓ cups water
   2 tablespoons vegetable oil
   1 cup coarsely chopped creme-filled chocolate sandwich cookies (about
      12 cookies)
   1 container DUNCAN HINES® Buttercream Frosting
      Additional cookies (optional)

**1.** Preheat oven to 350°F. Grease and flour two 9-inch round cake pans.

**2.** Combine cake mix, egg whites, water and oil in large mixing bowl. Beat at low speed with electric mixer until moistened. Beat at medium speed for 2 minutes. Fold in 1 cup cookies. Pour into prepared pans. Bake at 350°F for 28 to 31 minutes or until toothpick inserted in center comes out clean. Cool in pans 15 minutes. Remove from pans; cool completely. Fill and frost cake with frosting. Garnish with additional cookies, if desired. *Makes 12 to 16 servings*

**Hint:** To quickly chop cookies, place 6 cookies in food processor fitted with steel blade. Pulse several times until coarsely chopped. Repeat with remaining cookies.

## Strawberry Vanilla Cake

**1 package DUNCAN HINES® Moist Deluxe® French Vanilla Cake Mix**
**1 container DUNCAN HINES® Creamy Home-Style Classic Vanilla**
 **Frosting, divided**
**⅓ cup seedless strawberry jam**
 **Fresh strawberries for garnish (optional)**

**1.** Preheat oven to 350°F. Grease and flour two 8- or 9-inch round cake pans.

**2.** Prepare, bake and cool cake following package directions for basic recipe.

**3.** To assemble, place one cake layer on serving plate. Place ¼ cup frosting in small resealable plastic bag. Snip off one corner. Pipe bead of frosting on top of layer around outer edge. Fill remaining area with strawberry jam. Top with second cake layer. Spread remaining frosting on sides and top of cake. Decorate with fresh strawberries, if desired.                    ***Makes 12 to 16 servings***

## Mocha Fudge Cake

**1 package DUNCAN HINES® Moist Deluxe® Butter Recipe Fudge Cake**
 **Mix**
**1 cup hot fudge ice cream topping**
**1 tablespoon instant coffee granules**
**4 cups frozen non-dairy whipped topping, thawed, divided**

**1.** Preheat oven to 375°F. Grease and flour two 9-inch round cake pans.

**2.** Prepare, bake and cool cake as directed on package.

**3.** Combine hot fudge topping and coffee in medium saucepan. Heat until coffee crystals are dissolved. Cool. Fold 2 cups whipped topping into fudge topping mixture. Refrigerate 30 minutes.

**4.** Place one cake layer on serving plate. Spread with 1 cup filling. Top with second cake layer. Add remaining 2 cups whipped topping to remaining filling. Frost top and sides of cake with topping mixture.                    ***Makes 12 to 16 servings***

Strawberry Vanilla Cake

# Elegant Desserts

## Blueberry Angel Food Cake Rolls

1 package DUNCAN HINES® Angel Food Cake Mix
¼ cup confectioners' sugar plus additional for dusting
1 can (21 ounces) blueberry pie filling
Mint leaves for garnish (optional)

**1.** Preheat oven to 350°F. Line two 15½×10½×1-inch jelly-roll pans with aluminum foil.

**2.** Prepare cake mix as directed on package. Divide and spread evenly into prepared pans. Cut through batter with knife or spatula to remove large air bubbles. Bake at 350°F for 15 minutes or until set. Invert cakes at once onto clean, lint-free dishtowels dusted with confectioners' sugar. Remove foil carefully. Roll up each cake with towel jelly-roll fashion, starting at short end. Cool completely.

**3.** Unroll cakes. Spread about 1 cup blueberry pie filling to within 1 inch of edges on each cake. Reroll and place seam-side down on serving plate. Dust with ¼ cup sugar. Garnish with mint leaves, if desired.

*Makes 2 cakes (8 servings each)*

**Hint:** For a variation in flavor, substitute cherry pie filling for the blueberry pie filling.

## Trifle Spectacular

1 package Duncan Hines® Moist Deluxe® Devil's Food Cake Mix
1 can (14 ounces) sweetened condensed milk
1 cup cold water
1 package (4-serving size) vanilla-flavor instant pudding and pie filling mix
2 cups whipping cream, whipped
2 tablespoons orange juice, divided
2½ cups sliced fresh strawberries, divided
1 pint fresh raspberries, divided
2 kiwifruit, peeled and sliced, divided
1½ cups frozen whipped topping, thawed for garnish
Mint leaves for garnish (optional)

**1.** Preheat oven to 350°F. Grease and flour two 9-inch round cake pans.

**2.** Prepare, bake and cool cake following package directions for original recipe. Cut one cake layer into 1-inch cubes. Freeze other cake layer for later use.

**3.** Combine sweetened condensed milk and water in large bowl. Stir until blended. Add pudding mix. Beat until thoroughly blended. Chill 5 minutes. Fold whipped cream into pudding mixture.

**4.** To assemble, spread 2 cups pudding mixture into 3-quart trifle dish (or 3-quart clear glass bowl with straight sides). Arrange half the cake cubes over pudding mixture. Sprinkle with 1 tablespoon orange juice. Layer with 1 cup strawberry slices, half the raspberries and one-third of kiwifruit slices. Repeat layers. Top with remaining pudding mixture. Garnish with whipped topping, remaining ½ cup strawberry slices, kiwifruit slices and mint leaves, if desired.

*Makes 10 to 12 servings*

**Hint:** Since the different layers contribute to the beauty of this recipe, arrange the fruit pieces to show attractively along the sides of the trifle dish.

## Rich Pumpkin Cheesecake

*Crust*
   1 package DUNCAN HINES® Moist Deluxe® Spice Cake Mix
   ½ cup butter or margarine, melted

*Filling*
   3 packages (8 ounces each) cream cheese, softened
   1 can (14 ounces) sweetened condensed milk
   1 can (16 ounces) solid pack pumpkin
   4 eggs
   1 tablespoon pumpkin pie spice

*Topping*
   1 package (2½ ounces) sliced almonds
   2 cups whipping cream, chilled
   ¼ cup sugar

**1.** Preheat oven to 375°F.

**2.** For crust, combine cake mix and melted butter in large bowl; press onto bottom of ungreased 10-inch springform pan.

**3.** For filling, combine cream cheese and sweetened condensed milk in large bowl. Beat with electric mixer at high speed 2 minutes. Add pumpkin, eggs and pumpkin pie spice. Beat at high speed 1 minute. Pour over prepared crust in pan. Bake at 375°F for 65 to 70 minutes or until set. Cool completely on rack. Refrigerate 2 hours. Loosen cake from sides of pan; remove sides of pan.

**4.** For topping, preheat oven to 300°F. Toast almonds on ungreased baking sheet at 300°F for 4 to 5 minutes or until fragrant and light golden brown. Cool completely. Beat whipping cream in medium bowl with electric mixer at high speed until soft peaks form. Gradually add sugar; beat until stiff peaks form. Spread over top of chilled cake. Garnish with toasted almonds. Refrigerate until ready to serve.

*Makes 8 to 12 servings*

**Note:** To prepare this cheesecake in a 13×9×2-inch pan, bake at 350°F for 35 minutes or until set.

## Hot Fudge Sundae Cake

1 package DUNCAN HINES® Moist Deluxe® Dark Chocolate Fudge Cake
   Mix
½ gallon brick vanilla ice cream

*Fudge Sauce*
   1 can (12 ounces) evaporated milk
1¼ cups sugar
   4 squares (1 ounce each) unsweetened chocolate
¼ cup butter or margarine
1½ teaspoons vanilla extract
¼ teaspoon salt
   Whipped cream and maraschino cherries for garnish

**1.** Preheat oven to 350°F. Grease and flour 13×9×2-inch pan. Prepare, bake and cool cake following package directions.

**2.** Remove cake from pan. Split cake in half horizontally. Place bottom layer back in pan. Cut ice cream into even slices and place evenly over bottom cake layer (use all the ice cream). Place remaining cake layer over ice cream. Cover and freeze.

**3.** For fudge sauce, combine evaporated milk and sugar in medium saucepan. Stir constantly on medium heat until mixture comes to a rolling boil. Boil and stir for 1 minute. Add unsweetened chocolate and stir until melted. Beat over medium heat until smooth. Remove from heat. Stir in butter, vanilla extract and salt.

**4.** Cut cake into serving squares. For each serving, place cake square on plate; spoon hot fudge sauce on top. Garnish with whipped cream and maraschino cherry.

*Makes 12 to 16 servings*

**Note:** Fudge sauce can be prepared ahead and refrigerated in tightly sealed jar. Reheat when ready to serve.

## Tip

Store chocolate in a cool, dry place. If chocolate gets too warm, the cocoa butter rises to the surface and causes a grayish white appearance, which is called a bloom. The bloom will not affect the chocolate's taste or baking quality.

## Pears en Croûte (Baked Pears in Pastry)

2 teaspoons granulated sugar
¼ teaspoon ground cinnamon
1 egg white, lightly beaten
Cold water
¼ cup golden raisins
¼ cup chopped walnuts
2 tablespoons brown sugar
1 package DUNCAN HINES® Bakery-Style Cinnamon Muffin Mix
8 small ripe pears
1 cup all-purpose flour
½ cup shortening plus additional for greasing
Cinnamon sticks or vanilla beans for garnish
Caramel flavor topping, at room temperature or warmed

**1.** Preheat oven to 375°F. Grease 13×9×2-inch pan.

**2.** Combine granulated sugar and cinnamon in small bowl; set aside. Combine beaten egg white and 1 teaspoon water in small bowl; set aside.

**3.** Combine raisins, walnuts, brown sugar, cinnamon swirl packet from Mix and cinnamon topping packet from Mix in medium bowl; set aside.

**4.** Core and peel pears; set aside.

**5.** Combine muffin mix and flour in medium bowl. Cut in ½ cup shortening with pastry blender or 2 knives until flour is blended to form pea-size chunks. Sprinkle 5 tablespoons cold water, 1 tablespoon at a time, over flour mixture. Toss lightly with fork until dough forms ball. Divide in half. Wrap one half with plastic wrap; reserve. Roll remaining dough on well-floured surface to form 13-inch square. Cut square into four 6½-inch squares. Repeat using reserved dough ball.

**6.** To assemble, fill pear centers with 1½ tablespoons raisin mixture. Cover each pear with square of pastry. Mold with palm of hand to shape, folding corners under pear bottom. Place ¾ inch apart in prepared pan. Brush with egg white mixture. Sprinkle ¼ teaspoon cinnamon-sugar mixture over each pear.

**7.** Bake at 375°F for 33 to 35 minutes or until golden brown and pears are tender. Cool in pan for 5 minutes. Remove to serving dish. Insert cinnamon stick or piece of vanilla bean on top of pear to form stem. Drizzle caramel topping over pear, as desired. Serve warm or at room temperature. Refrigerate leftovers.

*Makes 8 servings*

**Hint:** For a pretty garnish, reroll leftover pastry and cut into small leaf shapes. Place on baking sheet. Bake at 375°F for 8 to 10 minutes.

Pear en Croûte (Baked Pear in Pastry)

## Boston Cream Pie

**1 package DUNCAN HINES® Moist Deluxe® Classic Yellow Cake Mix**
**4 containers (3½ ounces each) ready-to-eat vanilla pudding**
**1 container DUNCAN HINES® Chocolate Frosting**

**1.** Preheat oven to 350°F. Grease and flour two 8- or 9-inch round pans.

**2.** Prepare, bake and cool cake following package directions for basic recipe.

**3.** To assemble, place each cake layer on serving plate. Split layers in half horizontally. Spread contents of 2 containers of vanilla pudding on bottom layer of one cake. Place top layer on filling. Repeat for second cake layer. Remove lid and foil top of frosting container. Heat in microwave oven at HIGH (100% power) 25 to 30 seconds. Stir. (Mixture should be thin.) Spread half the chocolate glaze over top of each cake. Refrigerate until ready to serve. *Makes 12 to 16 servings*

**Hint:** For a richer flavor, substitute Duncan Hines® Butter Recipe Golden Cake Mix in place of Yellow cake mix.

## Cherries in the Snow Dessert

**1 package DUNCAN HINES® Angel Food Cake Mix**
**1 package (8 ounces) cream cheese, softened**
**1 cup confectioners' sugar**
**1 container (12 ounces) frozen whipped topping, thawed**
**1 can (21 ounces) cherry pie filling**

**1.** Preheat oven to 375°F. Prepare, bake and cool cake following package directions. Cut cake into 16 slices.

**2.** Combine cream cheese and confectioners' sugar in small bowl. Beat at medium speed with electric mixer until smooth.

**3.** To assemble, spread half the whipped topping in bottom of 13×9×2-inch pan. Arrange 8 cake slices on whipped topping; press lightly. Spread with cream cheese mixture. Arrange remaining cake slices on cream cheese mixture; press lightly. Spread with remaining whipped topping. Spoon cherry pie filling evenly over top. (Pan will be filled to the brim.) Refrigerate for 2 hours or until ready to serve. Cut into squares. *Makes 16 to 20 servings*

## Cranberry Cobbler

2 cans (16 ounces) sliced peaches in light syrup, drained
1 can (16 ounces) whole berry cranberry sauce
1 package DUNCAN HINES® Cinnamon Swirl Muffin Mix
½ cup chopped pecans
⅓ cup butter or margarine, melted
Whipped topping or ice cream

**1.** Preheat oven to 350°F.

**2.** Cut peach slices in half lengthwise. Combine peach slices and cranberry sauce in ungreased 9-inch square pan. Knead swirl packet from Mix for 10 seconds. Squeeze contents evenly over fruit.

**3.** Combine muffin mix, contents of topping packet from Mix and pecans in large bowl. Add melted butter. Stir until thoroughly blended (mixture will be crumbly). Sprinkle crumbs over fruit. Bake 40 to 45 minutes or until lightly browned and bubbly. Serve warm with whipped topping.          *Makes 9 servings*

**Note:** Store leftovers in the refrigerator. Reheat in microwave oven to serve warm.

## Butter Pecan Pie

1 cup coarsely chopped pecans
¼ cup butter or margarine
1 container DUNCAN HINES® Creamy Home-Style Buttercream Frosting
1 package (8 ounces) cream cheese, softened
1 cup frozen non-dairy whipped topping, thawed
1 prepared 9-inch graham cracker crumb pie crust
Pecan halves, for garnish

**1.** Place pecans and butter in 10-inch skillet on medium heat. Cook, stirring constantly, until butter is lightly browned. Pour into heat-proof large bowl. Add frosting and cream cheese. Stir until thoroughly blended.

**2.** Fold in whipped topping. Pour into prepared crust. Garnish with pecan halves, if desired. Refrigerate for 4 hours or until firm.          *Makes 8 to 10 servings*

## Angel Almond Cupcakes

    1 package DUNCAN HINES® Angel Food Cake Mix
1¼ cups water
    2 teaspoons almond extract
    1 container DUNCAN HINES® Wild Cherry Vanilla Frosting

**1.** Preheat oven to 350°F.

**2.** Combine cake mix, water and almond extract in large mixing bowl. Beat at low speed with electric mixer until moistened. Beat at medium speed for 1 minute. Line medium muffin pans with paper baking cups. Fill muffin cups two-thirds full. Bake at 350°F for 20 to 25 minutes or until golden brown, cracked and dry on top. Remove from muffin pans. Cool completely. Frost with frosting.

*Makes 30 to 32 cupcakes*

## Creamy Banana Toffee Dessert

    1 package DUNCAN HINES® Moist Deluxe® Butter Recipe Golden Cake
       Mix
    1 package (4-serving size) banana cream-flavor instant pudding and pie
       filling mix
1½ cups milk
    1 container (8 ounces) frozen non-dairy whipped topping, thawed
    3 medium bananas, sliced
    ¾ cup English toffee bits

**1.** Preheat oven to 375°F. Grease and flour 10-inch tube pan.

**2.** Prepare, bake and cool cake as directed on package. Meanwhile, combine pudding mix and milk in medium bowl. Chill 5 minutes. Fold in whipped topping. Chill while cake cools.

**3.** To assemble, cut cake into 12 slices. Place 6 cake slices in 3-quart clear glass bowl. Top with half of bananas, pudding and toffee bits. Repeat layering. Chill until ready to serve.

*Makes 12 to 14 servings*

## Chocolate Chip Cheesecake

1 package DUNCAN HINES® Moist Deluxe® Devil's Food Cake Mix
$\frac{1}{2}$ cup vegetable oil
3 packages (8 ounces each) cream cheese, softened
1$\frac{1}{2}$ cups granulated sugar
1 cup sour cream
1$\frac{1}{2}$ teaspoons vanilla extract
4 eggs, lightly beaten
$\frac{3}{4}$ cup mini semisweet chocolate chips, divided
1 teaspoon all-purpose flour

**1.** Preheat oven to 350°F. Grease 10-inch springform pan.

**2.** Combine cake mix and oil in large bowl. Mix well. Press onto bottom of prepared pan. Bake at 350°F for 22 to 25 minutes or until set. Remove from oven. *Increase oven temperature to 450°F.*

**3.** Place cream cheese in large mixing bowl. Beat at low speed with electric mixer, adding sugar gradually. Add sour cream and vanilla extract, mixing until blended. Add eggs, mixing only until incorporated. Toss $\frac{1}{2}$ cup chocolate chips with flour. Fold into cream cheese mixture. Pour filling onto crust. Sprinkle with remaining $\frac{1}{4}$ cup chocolate chips. Bake at 450°F for 5 to 7 minutes. *Reduce oven temperature to 250°F.* Bake at 250°F for 60 to 65 minutes or until set. Loosen cake from side of pan with knife or spatula. Cool completely in pan on cooling rack. Refrigerate until ready to serve. Remove side of pan. ***Makes 12 to 16 servings***

**Note:** Place a pan of water on the bottom shelf of the oven while baking to prevent the cheesecake from cracking.

### Tip

To soften cream cheese quickly, remove it from the wrapper and place it in a medium microwave-safe bowl. Microwave at MEDIUM (50% power) 15 to 20 seconds or until slightly softened. The softened cream cheese will combine more easily with the other ingredients which will prevent lumps from forming in the batter.

**Chocolate Chip Cheesecake**

## Strawberry Shortcake

*Cake*

> 1 package DUNCAN HINES® Moist Deluxe® French Vanilla Cake Mix
> 3 eggs
> 1¼ cups water
> ½ cup butter or margarine, softened

*Filling and Topping*

> 2 cups whipping cream, chilled
> ⅓ cup sugar
> ½ teaspoon vanilla extract
> 1 quart fresh strawberries, rinsed, drained and sliced
> Mint leaves for garnish

**1.** Preheat oven to 350°F. Grease two 9-inch round cake pans with butter or margarine. Sprinkle bottom and sides with granulated sugar.

**2.** For cake, combine cake mix, eggs, water and butter in large bowl. Beat at low speed with electric mixer until moistened. Beat at medium speed for 2 minutes. Pour into prepared pans. Bake at 350°F for 30 to 35 minutes or until toothpick inserted in center comes out clean. Cool in pan 10 minutes. Invert onto cooling rack. Cool completely.

**3.** For filling and topping, place whipping cream, sugar and vanilla extract in large bowl. Beat with electric mixer on high speed until stiff peaks form. Reserve ⅓ cup for garnish. Place one cake layer on serving plate. Spread with half of whipped cream and half of sliced strawberries. Place second layer on top of strawberries. Spread with remaining whipping cream and top with remaining strawberries. Dollop with reserved ½ cup whipped cream and garnish with mint leaves. Refrigerate until ready to serve.

*Makes 12 servings*

## Pumpkin Pie Crunch

  1 can (16 ounces) solid pack pumpkin
  1 can (12 ounces) evaporated milk
  3 eggs
1½ cups sugar
  4 teaspoons pumpkin pie spice
 ½ teaspoon salt
  1 package DUNCAN HINES® Moist Deluxe® Classic Yellow Cake Mix
  1 cup chopped pecans
  1 cup butter or margarine, melted
    Whipped topping

**1.** Preheat oven to 350°F. Grease bottom only of 13×9×2-inch pan.

**2.** Combine pumpkin, evaporated milk, eggs, sugar, pumpkin pie spice and salt in large bowl. Pour into prepared pan. Sprinkle dry cake mix evenly over pumpkin mixture. Top with pecans. Drizzle with melted butter. Bake at 350°F for 50 to 55 minutes or until golden. Cool completely. Serve with whipped topping. Refrigerate leftovers.
*Makes 16 to 20 servings*

**Hint:** For a richer flavor, try using Duncan Hines® Moist Deluxe® Butter Recipe Golden Cake Mix.

## Coconut Cupcakes

  1 package DUNCAN HINES® Moist Deluxe® Butter Recipe Golden
    Cake Mix
  3 eggs
  1 cup (8 ounces) dairy sour cream
⅔ cup cream of coconut
¼ cup butter or margarine, softened
  2 containers DUNCAN HINES® Coconut Frosting

**1.** Preheat oven to 375°F. Place 36 (2½-inch) paper liners in muffin cups.

**2.** Combine cake mix, eggs, sour cream, cream of coconut and butter in large bowl. Beat at low speed until blended. Beat at medium speed 4 minutes. Fill paper liners half full. Bake at 375°F for 17 to 19 minutes or until toothpick inserted in center comes out clean. Cool in pans 5 minutes. Remove to cooling racks. Cool completely.

**3.** Frost cupcakes.
*Makes 36 cupcakes*

## Cappuccino Bon Bons

1 package (21 ounces) **DUNCAN HINES®** Family-Style Chewy Fudge
    Brownie Mix
2 eggs
$\frac{1}{3}$ cup water
$\frac{1}{3}$ cup vegetable oil
$1\frac{1}{2}$ tablespoons instant coffee
1 teaspoon ground cinnamon
    Whipped topping
    Cinnamon

**1.** Preheat oven to 350°F. Place 2-inch foil cupcake liners on cookie sheet.

**2.** Combine brownie mix, eggs, water, oil, instant coffee and cinnamon. Stir with spoon until well blended, about 50 strokes. Fill each cupcake liner with 1 measuring tablespoon batter. Bake 12 to 15 minutes or until wooden toothpick inserted in center comes out clean. Cool completely. Garnish with whipped topping and a dash of cinnamon. Refrigerate until ready to serve.    ***Makes about 40 bon bons***

**Note:** To make larger bon bons, use twelve $2\frac{1}{2}$-inch foil cupcake liners and fill with $\frac{1}{4}$ cup batter. Bake 28 to 30 minutes.

### Tip

To measure liquid ingredients accurately, use a standardized glass or plastic measuring cup with a pouring spout. Place the cup on a flat surface, fill to the desired mark and check the measurement at eye level.

**Cappuccino Bon Bons**

## Strawberry Celebration Cake

**1 package DUNCAN HINES® Moist Deluxe® Strawberry Supreme Cake Mix**
**1 cup strawberry preserves, heated**
**1 container DUNCAN HINES® Creamy Home-Style Cream Cheese Frosting**
**Strawberry halves for garnish**
**Mint leaves for garnish**

**1.** Preheat oven to 350°F. Grease and flour 10-inch Bundt or tube pan.

**2.** Prepare, bake and cool cake following package directions for basic recipe.

**3.** Split cake horizontally into three even layers. Place bottom cake layer on serving plate. Spread with $1/2$ cup warm preserves. Repeat layering. Top with remaining cake layer. Frost cake with Cream Cheese frosting. Garnish with strawberry halves and mint leaves. Refrigerate until ready to serve.            ***Makes 12 to 16 servings***

**Hint:** For a delicious variation, substitute 1 cup seedless red raspberry jam for the strawberry preserves.

## Peachy Blueberry Crunch

**1 package DUNCAN HINES® Bakery-Style Blueberry Streusel Muffin Mix**
**4 cups sliced peeled peaches (about 4 large)**
**$1/2$ cup water**
**3 tablespoons packed brown sugar**
**$1/2$ cup chopped pecans**
**$1/3$ cup butter or margarine, melted**
**Whipped topping or ice cream (optional)**

**1.** Preheat oven to 350°F.

**2.** Rinse blueberries from Mix with cold water and drain.

**3.** Arrange peach slices in ungreased 9-inch square pan. Sprinkle blueberries over peaches. Combine water and sugar in small bowl. Pour over fruit.

**4.** Combine muffin mix, pecans and melted butter in large bowl. Stir until thoroughly blended (mixture will be crumbly). Sprinkle crumb mixture over fruit. Sprinkle contents of topping packet from Mix over crumb mixture. Bake at 350°F for 50 to 55 minutes or until lightly browned and bubbly. Serve warm with whipped topping, if desired.            ***Makes 9 servings***

**Strawberry Celebration Cake**

# Chocolate Treats

## Chocolate Peanut Butter Cups

1 package DUNCAN HINES® Moist Deluxe® Swiss Chocolate Cake Mix
1 container DUNCAN HINES® Creamy Home-Style Classic Vanilla Frosting
½ cup creamy peanut butter
15 miniature peanut butter cup candies, wrappers removed, cut in half vertically

**1.** Preheat oven to 350°F. Place 30 (2½-inch) paper liners in muffin cups.

**2.** Prepare, bake and cool cupcakes following package directions for basic recipe.

**3.** Combine Vanilla frosting and peanut butter in medium bowl. Stir until smooth. Frost one cupcake. Decorate with peanut butter cup candy, cut-side down. Repeat with remaining cupcakes, frosting and candies.

*Makes 30 servings*

**Hint:** You can substitute Duncan Hines® Moist Deluxe® Devil's Food, Dark Chocolate Fudge or Butter Recipe Fudge Cake Mix flavors for Swiss Chocolate Cake Mix.

## Chocolate Confection Cake

1 package DUNCAN HINES® Moist Deluxe® Devil's Food Cake Mix

*Filling*
1 cup evaporated milk
1 cup granulated sugar
24 large marshmallows
1 package (14 ounces) flaked coconut

*Topping*
$\frac{1}{2}$ cup butter or margarine
$\frac{1}{4}$ cup plus 2 tablespoons milk
$\frac{1}{3}$ cup unsweetened cocoa powder
1 pound confectioners' sugar ($3\frac{1}{2}$ to 4 cups)
1 teaspoon vanilla extract
$\frac{3}{4}$ cup sliced almonds

**1.** Preheat oven to 350°F. Grease and flour $15\frac{1}{2} \times 10\frac{1}{2} \times 1$-inch jelly-roll pan.

**2.** Prepare cake following package directions for original recipe. Pour into prepared pan. Bake at 350°F for 20 to 25 minutes or until toothpick inserted in center comes out clean.

**3.** For filling, combine evaporated milk and granulated sugar in large saucepan. Bring mixture to a boil. Add marshmallows and stir until melted. Stir in coconut. Spread on warm cake.

**4.** For topping, combine butter, milk and cocoa in medium saucepan. Stir on low heat until butter is melted. Add confectioners' sugar and vanilla extract, stirring until smooth. Stir in almonds (see Hint). Pour over filling. Spread evenly to edges. Cool completely.

*Makes 20 to 24 servings*

**Hint:** For a pretty presentation, sprinkle the $\frac{3}{4}$ cup almond slices over the topping instead of stirring them into the topping.

## Fudge Cake with Melba Topping

1 package DUNCAN HINES® Moist Deluxe® Dark Chocolate Fudge Cake
    Mix
   Egg substitute product equal to 3 eggs
1¼ cups water
½ cup vegetable oil

*Raspberry Sauce*
1 package (12 ounces) frozen dry pack raspberries, thawed, drained and
    juice reserved
½ cup sugar
2 teaspoons cornstarch
½ teaspoon grated lemon peel
1 can (29 ounces) sliced peaches in lite syrup, drained

**1.** Preheat oven to 350°F. Grease and flour 13×9×2-inch pan.

**2.** For cake, combine cake mix, egg substitute, water and oil in large bowl. Beat at medium speed with electric mixer for 2 minutes. Pour into prepared pan. Bake at 350°F for 35 to 40 minutes or until toothpick inserted in center comes out clean. Cool completely.

**3.** For sauce, combine reserved raspberry juice, sugar, cornstarch and lemon peel in medium saucepan. Bring to a boil. Reduce heat and cook until thickened, stirring constantly. Stir in reserved raspberries. Cool.

**4.** Cut cake into serving squares. Place several peach slices on top of cake square. Spoon raspberry sauce over peaches and cake. Serve immediately.

*Makes 20 servings*

### Tip

To separate the juice from the raspberries in one step, allow the berries to thaw at room temperature in a strainer placed over a bowl.

## Triple Chocolate Fantasy

*Cake*

   1 package DUNCAN HINES® Moist Deluxe® Devil's Food Cake Mix
   3 eggs
 1⅓ cups water
   ½ cup vegetable oil plus additional for greasing
   ½ cup ground walnuts

*Chocolate Glaze*

   1 package (12 ounces) semisweet chocolate chips
   ¼ cup plus 2 tablespoons butter or margarine
   ¼ cup coarsely chopped walnuts

*White Chocolate Glaze*

   3 ounces white chocolate, coarsely chopped
   1 tablespoon shortening

**1.** Preheat oven to 350°F. Grease and flour 10-inch Bundt pan.

**2.** For cake, combine cake mix, eggs, water, oil and ground walnuts in large bowl. Beat at medium speed with electric mixer for 2 minutes. Pour into prepared pan. Bake at 350°F for 45 to 55 minutes or until toothpick inserted in center comes out clean. Cool in pan 25 minutes. Invert onto serving plate. Cool completely.

**3.** For chocolate glaze, combine chocolate chips and butter in small heavy saucepan. Heat on low heat until chips are melted. Stir constantly until shiny and smooth. (Glaze will be very thick.) Spread hot glaze over cooled cake. Sprinkle with coarsely chopped walnuts.

**4.** For white chocolate glaze, combine white chocolate and shortening in small heavy saucepan. Heat on low heat until melted, stirring constantly. Drizzle hot glaze over top and sides of cake.                              *Makes 12 to 16 servings*

## Black Forest Torte

1 package DUNCAN HINES® Moist Deluxe® Dark Chocolate Fudge Cake
   Mix
2½ cups whipping cream, chilled
2½ tablespoons confectioners' sugar
1 can (21 ounces) cherry pie filling

**1.** Preheat oven to 350°F. Grease and flour two 9-inch round cake pans.

**2.** Prepare, bake and cool cake as directed on package.

**3.** Beat whipping cream in large bowl until soft peaks form. Add sugar gradually. Beat until stiff peaks form.

**4.** To assemble, place one cake layer on serving plate. Spread two-thirds cherry pie filling on cake to within ½ inch of edge. Spread 1½ cups whipped cream mixture over cherry pie filling. Top with second cake layer. Frost sides and top with remaining whipped cream mixture. Spread remaining cherry pie filling on top to within 1 inch of edge. Refrigerate until ready to serve.            *Makes 12 to 16 servings*

**Hint:** Chill the cherry pie filling for easy spreading on the cake. Also, garnish the cake with grated semisweet chocolate or white chocolate curls.

## Swiss Chocolate Crispies

1 package DUNCAN HINES® Moist Deluxe® Swiss Chocolate Cake Mix
½ cup shortening plus additional for greasing
½ cup butter or margarine, softened
2 eggs
2 tablespoons water
3 cups crispy rice cereal, divided

**1.** Combine cake mix, ½ cup shortening, butter, eggs and water in large bowl. Beat at low speed with electric mixer for 2 minutes. Fold in 1 cup cereal. Refrigerate 1 hour.

**2.** Crush remaining 2 cups cereal into coarse crumbs.

**3.** Preheat oven to 350°F. Grease baking sheets. Shape dough into 1-inch balls. Roll in crushed cereal. Place on baking sheets about 1 inch apart.

**4.** Bake at 350°F for 11 to 13 minutes. Cool 1 minute on baking sheets. Remove to wire racks.            *Makes about 4 dozen cookies*

**Black Forest Torte**

## Chocolate Petits Fours

1 package DUNCAN HINES® Moist Deluxe® Dark Chocolate Fudge Cake
   Mix
1 package (7 ounces) pure almond paste
$^1/_2$ cup seedless red raspberry jam
3 cups semisweet chocolate chips
$^1/_2$ cup vegetable shortening plus additional for greasing

**1.** Preheat oven to 350°F. Grease and flour 13×9×2-inch pan.

**2.** Prepare, bake and cool cake following package directions for basic recipe. Remove
from pan. Cover and store overnight (see Note). Level top of cake. Trim $^1/_4$-inch strip
of cake from all sides. (Be careful to make straight cuts.) Cut cake into small squares,
rectangles or triangles with serrated knife. Cut round and heart shapes with $1^1/_2$- to
2-inch cookie cutters. Split each individual cake horizontally into two layers.

**3.** For filling, cut almond paste in half. Roll half the paste between two sheets of
waxed paper to $^1/_8$-inch thickness. Cut into same shapes as individual cakes. Repeat
with second half of paste. Warm jam in small saucepan over low heat until thin.
Remove top of one cake. Spread $^1/_4$ to $^1/_2$ teaspoon jam on inside of each cut surface.
Place one almond paste cutout on bottom layer. Top with second half of cake, jam
side down. Repeat with remaining cakes.

**4.** For glaze, place chocolate chips and $^1/_2$ cup shortening in 4-cup glass measuring
cup. Microwave at MEDIUM (50% power) for 2 minutes; stir. Microwave for
2 minutes longer at MEDIUM; stir until smooth. Place 3 assembled cakes on cooling
rack over bowl. Spoon chocolate glaze over each cake until top and sides are
completely covered. Remove to waxed paper when glaze has stopped dripping.
Repeat process until all cakes are covered. (Return chocolate glaze in bowl to glass
measuring cup as needed; microwave at MEDIUM for 30 to 60 seconds to thin.)

**5.** Place remaining chocolate glaze in resealable plastic bag; seal. Place bag in bowl of
hot water for several minutes. Dry with paper towel. Knead until chocolate is smooth.
Snip pinpoint hole in bottom corner of bag. Drizzle or decorate top of each petit
four. Let stand until chocolate is set. Store in single layer in airtight containers.

***Makes 24 to 32 servings***

**Note:** To make cutting the cake into shapes easier, bake the cake one day before
assembling.

## Double Chocolate Snack Cake

**1 package DUNCAN HINES® Moist Deluxe® Devil's Food Cake Mix**
**1 cup white chocolate chips, divided**
**½ cup semisweet chocolate chips**

**1.** Preheat oven to 350°F. Grease and flour 13×9-inch pan.

**2.** Prepare cake mix as directed on package. Stir in ½ cup white chocolate chips and semisweet chocolate chips. Pour into prepared pan. Bake at 350°F for 35 to 40 minutes or until toothpick inserted in center comes out clean. Remove from oven; sprinkle top with remaining ½ cup white chocolate chips. Serve warm or cool completely in pan.

*Makes 12 to 16 servings*

**Hint:** For a special dessert, serve this cake warm with a scoop of vanilla ice cream or whipped cream garnished with chocolate chips.

## Triple Chocolate Cookies

**1 package DUNCAN HINES® Moist Deluxe® Swiss Chocolate Cake Mix**
**½ cup butter or margarine, melted**
**1 egg**
**½ cup semisweet chocolate chips**
**½ cup milk chocolate chips**
**½ cup coarsely chopped white chocolate**
**½ cup chopped pecans**

**1.** Preheat oven to 375°F.

**2.** Combine cake mix, melted butter and egg in large bowl. Beat at low speed with electric mixer until blended. Stir in all 3 chocolates and pecans.

**3.** Drop by rounded tablespoonfuls onto ungreased baking sheets. Bake at 375°F for 9 to 11 minutes. Cool 1 minute on baking sheet. Remove to cooling racks.

*Makes 3½ to 4 dozen cookies*

**Note:** These cookies may be stored in an airtight container in the freezer for up to 6 months.

## Brownie Ice Cream Pie

1 package (21 ounces) DUNCAN HINES® Chewy Fudge Brownie Mix
2 eggs
½ cup vegetable oil
¼ cup water
¾ cup semisweet chocolate chips
1 unbaked (9-inch) pastry crust
1 package (10 ounces) frozen sweetened sliced strawberries
   Vanilla ice cream

**1.** Preheat oven to 350°F.

**2.** Combine brownie mix, eggs, oil and water in large bowl. Stir with spoon until well blended, about 50 strokes. Stir in chocolate chips. Spoon into crust. Bake at 350°F for 40 to 45 minutes or until set. Cool completely. Purée strawberries in food processor or blender. Cut pie into wedges. Serve with ice cream and puréed strawberries.

*Makes 8 servings*

## Truffles

1 container DUNCAN HINES® Creamy Home-Style Milk Chocolate
   Frosting
2½ cups confectioners' sugar
1 cup pecan halves, divided
1 cup semisweet chocolate chips
3 tablespoons shortening

**1.** Combine frosting and sugar in large mixing bowl. Stir with wooden spoon until thoroughly blended. Chop ⅓ cup pecan halves; set aside. Cover remaining pecan halves with 1 tablespoon frosting mixture each. Roll into 1-inch balls; set aside.

**2.** Place chocolate chips and shortening in 2-cup glass measuring cup. Microwave at MEDIUM (50% power) for 2 minutes; stir. Microwave 1 minute at MEDIUM; stir until smooth. Dip one candy ball into chocolate mixture until completely covered. Remove with fork to cooling rack. Sprinkle top with chopped pecans. Repeat until all candy balls are covered. Allow to stand until chocolate mixture is set.

*Makes about 3 dozen candies*

## Chocolate Dream Torte

1 package DUNCAN HINES® Moist Deluxe® Dark Chocolate Fudge Cake
   Mix
1 package (6 ounces) semisweet chocolate chips, melted
1 container (8 ounces) frozen non-dairy whipped topping, thawed,
   divided
1 container DUNCAN HINES® Creamy Home-Style Milk Chocolate
   Frosting
3 tablespoons finely chopped dry roasted pistachios

**1.** Preheat oven to 350°F. Grease and flour two 9-inch round cake pans.

**2.** Prepare, bake and cool cake as directed on package for basic recipe.

**3.** For chocolate hearts garnish, spread melted chocolate to $\frac{1}{8}$-inch thickness on waxed paper-lined baking sheet. Cut shapes with heart cookie cutter when chocolate begins to set. Refrigerate until firm. Push out heart shapes. Set aside.

**4.** To assemble, split each cake layer in half horizontally. Place one split cake layer on serving plate. Spread one-third of whipped topping on top. Repeat with remaining layers and whipped topping, leaving top plain. Frost sides and top with frosting. Sprinkle pistachios on top. Position chocolate hearts by pushing points down into cake. Refrigerate until ready to serve.                          *Makes 12 to 16 servings*

**Chocolate Strawberry Dream Torte:** Omit semisweet chocolate chips and chopped pistachios. Proceed as directed through step 2. Fold $1\frac{1}{2}$ cups chopped fresh strawberries into whipped topping in large bowl. Assemble as directed, filling torte with strawberry mixture and frosting with Milk Chocolate frosting. Garnish cake with strawberry fans and mint leaves, if desired.

### Tip

When melting chocolate, make sure that all of your utensils are completely dry. Moisture, whether from utensils or a drop of water, may cause chocolate to become stiff and grainy. If this happens, try adding $\frac{1}{2}$ teaspoon of shortening (not butter or margarine, which contain water) for each ounce of chocolate and stir until smooth.

# Just for Kids

## Turtle Cake

1 package DUNCAN HINES® Moist Deluxe® Fudge Marble Cake
   Mix
6 fun-size chocolate-covered nougat, caramel, peanut candy bars
1 container DUNCAN HINES® Creamy Home-Style Cream Cheese
   Frosting, divided
   Green food coloring
2 tablespoons slivered almonds
   Candy-coated chocolate pieces
   White chocolate chips

**1.** Preheat oven to 350°F. Grease and flour 2$^{1}/_{2}$-quart ovenproof glass bowl with rounded bottom.

**2.** Prepare cake following package directions for original recipe. Pour into prepared bowl. Bake at 350°F for 55 to 60 minutes or until toothpick inserted in center comes out clean. Cool in bowl 20 minutes. Invert onto cooling rack. Cool completely.

**3.** Place cake on serving plate. Remove 1-inch cake square from upper side of cake for head. Insert 2 fun-size candy bars, flat sides together, into square hole for head. Position remaining 4 candy bars under cake for feet. Reserve 1 teaspoon Cream Cheese frosting. Tint remaining Cream Cheese frosting with green food coloring; frost cake. Sprinkle almonds on top. Place candy-coated chocolate pieces around bottom edge of shell. Attach white chocolate chips to head with reserved frosting for eyes. ***Makes 12 to 16 servings***

## Banana Split Cake

1 package DUNCAN HINES® Moist Deluxe® Banana Supreme Cake Mix

3 eggs

1⅓ cups water

½ cup all-purpose flour

⅓ cup vegetable oil

1 cup mini semisweet chocolate chips

2 to 3 bananas

1 can (16 ounces) chocolate syrup

1 container (8 ounces) frozen whipped topping, thawed

½ cup chopped walnuts

Colored sprinkles

Maraschino cherries with stems for garnish

**1.** Preheat oven to 350°F. Grease and flour 13×9×2-inch pan.

**2.** Combine cake mix, eggs, water, flour and oil in large bowl. Beat at low speed with electric mixer until moistened. Beat at medium speed 2 minutes. Stir in chocolate chips. Pour into prepared pan. Bake at 350°F for 32 to 35 minutes or until toothpick inserted in center comes out clean. Cool completely.

**3.** Slice bananas. Cut cake into squares; top with banana slices. Drizzle with chocolate syrup. Top with whipped topping, walnuts and sprinkles. Garnish with maraschino cherries.

*Makes 12 to 16 servings*

**Hint:** Dip bananas in diluted lemon juice to prevent darkening.

## Captivating Caterpillar Cupcakes

1 package DUNCAN HINES® Moist Deluxe® White Cake Mix
3 egg whites
1⅓ cups water
2 tablespoons vegetable oil
½ cup star decors, divided
1 container DUNCAN HINES® Vanilla Frosting
Green food coloring
6 chocolate sandwich cookies, finely crushed (see Hint)
½ cup candy-coated chocolate pieces
⅓ cup assorted jelly beans
Assorted nonpareil decors

**1.** Preheat oven to 350°F. Place 24 (2½-inch) paper liners in muffin cups.

**2.** Combine cake mix, egg whites, water and oil in large bowl. Beat at low speed with electric mixer until moistened. Beat at medium speed 2 minutes. Fold in ⅓ cup star decors. Fill paper liners about half full. Bake at 350°F for 18 to 23 minutes or until toothpick inserted in center comes out clean. Cool in pans 5 minutes. Remove to cooling racks. Cool completely.

**3.** Tint Vanilla frosting with green food coloring. Frost one cupcake. Sprinkle ½ teaspoon chocolate cookie crumbs on frosting. Arrange 4 candy-coated chocolate pieces to form caterpillar body. Place jelly bean at one end to form head. Attach remaining star and nonpareil decors with dots of frosting to form eyes. Repeat with remaining cupcakes. *Makes 24 cupcakes*

**Hint:** To finely crush chocolate sandwich cookies, place cookies in resealable plastic bag. Remove excess air from bag; seal. Press rolling pin on top of cookies to break into pieces. Continue pressing until evenly crushed.

## Ice Cream Cookie Sandwich

**2 pints chocolate chip ice cream, softened
1 package DUNCAN HINES® Moist Deluxe® Dark Chocolate Fudge Cake
   Mix
½ cup butter or margarine, softened**

**1.** Line bottom of one 9-inch round cake pan with aluminum foil. Spread ice cream in pan; return to freezer until firm. Run knife around edge of pan to loosen ice cream. Remove from pan; wrap in foil and return to freezer.

**2.** Preheat oven to 350°F. Line bottom of two 9-inch round cake pans with aluminum foil. Place cake mix in large bowl. Add butter; mix thoroughly until crumbs form. Place half the cake mix in each prepared pan; press lightly. Bake at 350°F for 15 minutes or until browned around edges; do not overbake. Cool 10 minutes; remove from pans. Remove foil from cookie layers; cool completely.

**3.** To assemble, place one cookie layer on serving plate. Top with ice cream. Peel off foil. Place second cookie layer on top. Wrap in foil and freeze 2 hours. To keep longer, store in airtight container. Let stand at room temperature for 5 to 10 minutes before cutting.                                     ***Makes 10 to 12 servings***

## Clown Cupcakes

**1 package DUNCAN HINES® Moist Deluxe® Classic Yellow Cake Mix
12 scoops vanilla ice cream
12 sugar ice cream cones
1 container (7 ounces) refrigerated aerosol whipped cream
   Assorted colored decors
   Assorted candies for eyes, nose and mouth**

**1.** Preheat oven to 350°F. Place 2½-inch paper liners in 24 muffin cups.

**2.** Prepare, bake and cool cupcakes following package directions.

**3.** Remove paper from 12 cupcakes. Place top-side down on serving plates. Top with scoops of ice cream. Place cones on ice cream for hats. Spray whipped cream around bottom of cupcakes for collar. Spray three small dots up front on cones. Sprinkle whipped cream with assorted colored decors. Use candies to make clowns' faces.                                     ***Makes 12 clown cupcakes***

**Note:** This recipe makes 24 cupcakes: 12 to make into "clowns" and 12 to freeze for later use.

## Brownie Gems

1 package DUNCAN HINES® Chocolate Lover's® Double Fudge Brownie
　Mix
2 eggs
2 tablespoons water
⅓ cup vegetable oil
28 miniature peanut butter cup or chocolate kiss candies
1 container of your favorite Duncan Hines frosting

**1.** Preheat oven to 350°F. Spray (1¾-inch) mini-muffin pans with vegetable cooking spray or line with foil baking cups.

**2.** Combine brownie mix, fudge packet from Mix, eggs, water and oil in large bowl. Stir with spoon until well blended, about 50 strokes. Drop 1 heaping teaspoonful of batter into each muffin cup; top with candy. Cover candy with more batter. Bake at 350°F for 15 to 17 minutes.

**3.** Cool 5 minutes. Carefully loosen brownies from pan. Remove to cool completely. Frost and decorate as desired.　　　　　*Makes 30 brownie gems*

### Tip

Refrigerate eggs immediately after purchasing. To prevent them from absorbing odors from other foods, store them in the original carton. For best flavor, use eggs within a week after purchasing. However, they will keep for up to five weeks after the packing date without loss of nutrients or functional properties.

## Football Cake

**1 package DUNCAN HINES® Moist Deluxe® Devil's Food Cake Mix**

*Decorator Frosting*
**¾ cup confectioners' sugar**
**2 tablespoons shortening plus additional for greasing**
**1 tablespoon cold water**
**1 tablespoon non-dairy powdered creamer**
**¼ teaspoon vanilla extract**
**Dash salt**
**1 container DUNCAN HINES® Creamy Home-Style Chocolate Frosting**

**1.** Preheat oven to 350°F. Grease and flour 10-inch round cake pan. Prepare cake following package directions for basic recipe. Bake at 350°F for 45 to 55 minutes or until toothpick inserted in center comes out clean.

**2.** For decorator frosting, combine confectioners' sugar, shortening, water, non-dairy powdered creamer, vanilla extract and salt in small bowl. Beat at medium speed with electric mixer 2 minutes. Add more confectioners' sugar to thicken or water to thin frosting as needed.

**3.** Cut cake and remove 2-inch slice from center. Arrange cake as shown. Spread chocolate frosting on sides and top of cake. Place basketweave tip in pastry bag. Fill with decorator frosting. Make white frosting laces on football.

*Makes 12 to 16 servings*

**Note:** If a 10-inch round pan is not available, make 2 football cakes by following package directions for baking with two 9-inch round cake pans.

## Kids' Confetti Cake

*Cake*

    1 package DUNCAN HINES® Moist Deluxe® Classic Yellow Cake Mix
    1 package (4-serving size) vanilla-flavor instant pudding and pie filling
       mix
    4 eggs
    1 cup water
    ½ cup vegetable oil
    1 cup mini semisweet chocolate chips

*Topping*

    1 cup colored mini marshmallows
    ⅔ cup DUNCAN HINES® Creamy Home-Style Chocolate Frosting
    2 tablespoons mini semisweet chocolate chips

**1.** Preheat oven to 350°F. Grease and flour 13×9×2-inch baking pan.

**2.** For cake, combine cake mix, pudding mix, eggs, water and oil in large bowl. Beat at medium speed with electric mixer 2 minutes. Stir in 1 cup chocolate chips. Pour into prepared pan. Bake at 350°F for 40 to 45 minutes or until toothpick inserted in center comes out clean.

**3.** For topping, immediately arrange marshmallows evenly over hot cake. Place frosting in microwave-safe bowl. Microwave at HIGH (100% power) 25 to 30 seconds. Stir until smooth. Drizzle evenly over marshmallows and cake. Sprinkle with 2 tablespoons chocolate chips. Cool completely.    ***Makes 12 to 16 servings***

## Porcupine Cupcakes

    1 package DUNCAN HINES® Moist Deluxe® Cake Mix (any flavor)
    1 container DUNCAN HINES® Chocolate Frosting
    Sliced almonds

**1.** Preheat oven to 350°F. Place 2½-inch paper liners in 24 muffin cups.

**2.** Prepare, bake and cool cupcakes following package directions for basic recipe. Frost cupcakes with Chocolate frosting. Place sliced almonds upright on each cupcake to decorate as a "porcupine."    ***Makes 24 cupcakes***

**Note:** Slivered almonds can be used in place of sliced almonds.

## Ice Cream Cone Cakes

1 package DUNCAN HINES® Moist Deluxe® Cake Mix (any flavor)
1 container DUNCAN HINES® Creamy Home-Style Chocolate Frosting
1 container DUNCAN HINES® Creamy Home-Style Vanilla Frosting
   Chocolate sprinkles
   Assorted decors
   Jelly beans
2 maraschino cherries for garnish

**1.** Preheat oven to 350°F. Grease and flour one 8-inch round cake pan and one 8-inch square pan.

**2.** Prepare cake following package directions for basic recipe. Pour about 2 cups batter into round pan. Pour about 3 cups batter into square pan. Bake at 350°F for 30 to 35 minutes or until toothpicks inserted in centers come out clean. Cool following package directions.

**3.** To assemble, cut cooled cake and arrange as shown. Frost "cone" with Chocolate frosting, reserving $1/2$ cup. Place writing tip in pastry bag. Fill with remaining $1/2$ cup Chocolate frosting. Pipe waffle pattern onto "cones." Decorate with chocolate sprinkles. Spread Vanilla frosting on "ice cream." Decorate with assorted decors and jelly beans. Top each with maraschino cherry.    ***Makes 12 to 16 servings***

**Hint:** Use tip of knife to draw lines in frosting for waffle pattern as guide for piping chocolate frosting.

## Candy Bar Brownies

1 package (21 ounces) DUNCAN HINES® Family-Style Chewy Fudge
   Brownie Mix
4 bars (5.3 ounces each) milk chocolate candy bars
$1/3$ cup mini candy-coated milk chocolate pieces

**1.** Preheat oven to 350°F. Grease bottom only of 13×9×2-inch pan.

**2.** Prepare and bake brownies following package directions for basic recipe chewy brownies. Break chocolate candy bars along scored lines. Place pieces immediately on hot brownies. Cover pan with aluminum foil for 3 to 5 minutes or until chocolate is shiny and soft. Spread gently to cover surface of brownies. Sprinkle with candy-coated chocolate pieces. Cool completely. Cut into bars.    ***Makes 18 brownies***

**Hint:** For another delicious candy topping, try sprinkling melted chocolate with $1/2$ cup chopped chocolate-covered toffee chips.

## Chocolate Bunny Cookies

1 package (21 ounces) DUNCAN HINES® Family-Style Chewy Fudge
   Brownie Mix
1 egg
¼ cup water
¼ cup vegetable oil
1⅓ cups pecan halves (96)
1 container DUNCAN HINES® Creamy Home-Style Dark Chocolate
   Fudge Frosting
White chocolate chips

**1.** Preheat oven to 350°F. Grease baking sheets.

**2.** Combine brownie mix, egg, water and oil in large bowl. Stir with spoon until well blended, about 50 strokes. Drop by 2 level teaspoonfuls 2 inches apart on greased baking sheets. Place two pecan halves, flat-side up, on each cookie for ears. Bake at 350°F for 10 to 12 minutes or until set. Cool 2 minutes on baking sheets. Remove to cooling racks. Cool completely.

**3.** Spread Dark Chocolate Fudge frosting on one cookie. Place white chocolate chips, upside down, on frosting for eyes and nose. Dot each eye with frosting using toothpick. Repeat for remaining cookies. Allow frosting to set before storing cookies between layers of waxed paper in airtight container.　　*Makes 4 dozen cookies*

**Hint:** For variety, frost cookies with Duncan Hines® Vanilla Frosting and use semisweet chocolate chips for the eyes and noses.

### Tip
Most cookies bake quickly and should be watched carefully to avoid overbaking. Check them at the minimum baking time, then watch carefully to make sure they don't burn. It is generally better to slightly underbake rather than to overbake cookies.

## Chocolate Chip Waffles

1 package DUNCAN HINES® Chocolate Chip Muffin Mix
¾ cup all-purpose flour
1 teaspoon baking powder
1¾ cups milk
2 eggs
5 tablespoons butter or margarine, melted
Confectioners' sugar (optional)

1. Preheat and lightly grease waffle iron according to manufacturer's directions.

2. Combine muffin mix, flour and baking powder in large bowl. Add milk, eggs and melted butter. Stir until moistened, about 50 strokes. Pour batter onto center grids of preheated waffle iron. Bake according to manufacturer's directions until golden brown. Remove baked waffle carefully with fork. Repeat with remaining batter. Dust lightly with sugar, if desired. Top with fresh fruit, syrup, grated chocolate or whipped cream, if desired.

*Makes 10 to 12 waffles*

## Brownie Sundaes for Kids

½ gallon vanilla ice cream
Assorted decors
Chopped nuts
1 package DUNCAN HINES® Double Fudge Brownie Mix
2 eggs
⅓ cup water
¼ cup vegetable oil
Hot fudge ice cream topping, heated

1. Preheat oven to 350°F. Line baking sheet with waxed paper. Grease bottom only of 8×8-inch pan.

2. Scoop ice cream into balls; place on lined baking sheet. Sprinkle each ice cream ball heavily with assorted decors or chopped nuts. Place in freezer until ready to serve.

3. Combine brownie mix, fudge packet from Mix, eggs, water and oil in large bowl. Stir with spoon until well blended, about 50 strokes. Pour into prepared pan. Bake at 350°F for 35 to 38 minutes or until set. Cool completely.

4. To assemble, cut brownies into 9 squares. Place on serving plates. Spoon hot fudge topping on top of each brownie square. Arrange garnished ice cream ball on each square. Serve immediately.

*Makes 9 brownie sundaes*

## Chocolate Peanut Butter Cookies

1 package DUNCAN HINES® Moist Deluxe® Devil's Food Cake Mix
¾ cup crunchy peanut butter
2 eggs
2 tablespoons milk
1 cup candy-coated peanut butter pieces

**1.** Preheat oven to 350°F. Grease baking sheets.

**2.** Combine cake mix, peanut butter, eggs and milk in large mixing bowl. Beat at low speed with electric mixer until blended. Stir in peanut butter pieces.

**3.** Drop dough by slightly rounded tablespoonfuls onto prepared baking sheets. Bake at 350°F for 7 to 9 minutes or until lightly browned. Cool 2 minutes on baking sheets. Remove to cooling racks.          *Makes about 3½ dozen cookies*

**Hint:** You can use 1 cup peanut butter chips in place of peanut butter pieces.

## Choco-Scutterbotch

⅔ cup shortening
½ cup firmly packed brown sugar
2 eggs
1 package DUNCAN HINES® Moist Deluxe® Classic Yellow Cake Mix
1 cup toasted rice cereal
½ cup milk chocolate chips
½ cup semisweet chocolate chips
½ cup butterscotch flavored chips
½ cup coarsely chopped walnuts or pecans

**1.** Preheat oven to 375°F.

**2.** Combine ⅔ cup shortening and brown sugar in large bowl. Beat at medium speed of electric mixer until well blended. Beat in eggs.

**3.** Add yellow cake mix gradually at low speed. Mix until well blended. Stir in cereal, both kinds of chocolate chips, butterscotch chips and walnuts with spoon. Stir until well blended. Shape dough into 1¼-inch balls. Place 2 inches apart on ungreased baking sheets. Flatten slightly to form circles.

**4.** Bake at 375°F for 7 to 9 minutes or until lightly browned around edges. Cool 2 minutes before removing to wire racks.          *Makes about 3 dozen cookies*

## Back-To-School Pencil Cake

**1 package DUNCAN HINES® Moist Deluxe® Cake Mix (any flavor)**
**2 containers DUNCAN HINES® Creamy Home-Style Classic Vanilla**
    **Frosting, divided**
**Red and yellow food coloring**
**Chocolate sprinkles**

**1.** Preheat oven to 350°F. Grease and flour 13×9×2-inch pan.

**2.** Prepare, bake and cool cake following package directions for basic recipe.

**3.** For frosting, tint 1 cup Vanilla frosting pink with red food coloring. Tint remaining frosting with yellow food coloring.

**4.** To assemble, cut cooled cake and arrange on large baking sheet or piece of sturdy cardboard as shown. Spread pink frosting on cake for eraser at one end and for wood at other end. Spread yellow frosting over remaining cake. Decorate with chocolate sprinkles for pencil tip and eraser band (see photo).     *Makes 12 to 16 servings*

**Hint:** To make this cake even more special, reserve ¼ cup Vanilla frosting before tinting yellow. Place writing tip in decorating bag. Fill with frosting. Pipe name of child, teacher or school on pencil.

### Tip

Make sure the cake is completely cool before frosting it. Brush off any loose crumbs from the cake's surface. To keep the cake plate clean, place small pieces of waxed paper under the edges of the cake; remove them after the cake has been frosted. For best results, use a flat metal spatula for applying frosting.

## Berry Surprise Cupcakes

1 package DUNCAN HINES® Moist Deluxe® White Cake Mix
3 egg whites
1⅓ cups water
2 tablespoons vegetable oil
3 sheets (0.5 ounce each) strawberry chewy fruit snacks
1 container DUNCAN HINES® Vanilla Frosting
2 pouches (0.9 ounce each) chewy fruit snack shapes for garnish (optional)

**1.** Preheat oven to 350°F. Place 24 (2½-inch) paper liners in muffin cups.

**2.** Combine cake mix, egg whites, water and oil in large bowl. Beat at low speed with electric mixer until moistened. Beat at medium speed 2 minutes. Fill each liner half full with batter.

**3.** Cut three fruit snack sheets into 9 equal pieces. (You will have 3 extra squares.) Place each fruit snack piece on top of batter in each cup. Pour remaining batter equally over each. Bake at 350°F for 18 to 23 minutes or until toothpick inserted in center comes out clean. Cool in pans 5 minutes. Remove to cooling racks. Cool completely. Frost cupcakes with Vanilla frosting. Decorate with fruit snack shapes, if desired.               ***Makes 12 to 16 servings***

**Variation:** To make a Berry Surprise Cake, prepare cake following package directions. Pour half the batter into prepared 13×9×2-inch pan. Place 4 fruit snack sheets evenly on top. Pour remaining batter over all. Bake and cool as directed on package. Frost and decorate as described above.

# *Index*

# METRIC CONVERSION CHART

### VOLUME MEASUREMENTS (dry)

1/8 teaspoon = 0.5 mL
1/4 teaspoon = 1 mL
1/2 teaspoon = 2 mL
3/4 teaspoon = 4 mL
1 teaspoon = 5 mL
1 tablespoon = 15 mL
2 tablespoons = 30 mL
1/4 cup = 60 mL
1/3 cup = 75 mL
1/2 cup = 125 mL
2/3 cup = 150 mL
3/4 cup = 175 mL
1 cup = 250 mL
2 cups = 1 pint = 500 mL
3 cups = 750 mL
4 cups = 1 quart = 1 L

### VOLUME MEASUREMENTS (fluid)

1 fluid ounce (2 tablespoons) = 30 mL
4 fluid ounces (1/2 cup) = 125 mL
8 fluid ounces (1 cup) = 250 mL
12 fluid ounces (1 1/2 cups) = 375 mL
16 fluid ounces (2 cups) = 500 mL

### WEIGHTS (mass)

1/2 ounce = 15 g
1 ounce = 30 g
3 ounces = 90 g
4 ounces = 120 g
8 ounces = 225 g
10 ounces = 285 g
12 ounces = 360 g
16 ounces = 1 pound = 450 g

### DIMENSIONS

1/16 inch = 2 mm
1/8 inch = 3 mm
1/4 inch = 6 mm
1/2 inch = 1.5 cm
3/4 inch = 2 cm
1 inch = 2.5 cm

### OVEN TEMPERATURES

250°F = 120°C
275°F = 140°C
300°F = 150°C
325°F = 160°C
350°F = 180°C
375°F = 190°C
400°F = 200°C
425°F = 220°C
450°F = 230°C

### BAKING PAN SIZES

| Utensil | Size in Inches/Quarts | Metric Volume | Size in Centimeters |
|---|---|---|---|
| Baking or Cake Pan (square or rectangular) | 8×8×2 | 2 L | 20×20×5 |
| | 9×9×2 | 2.5 L | 23×23×5 |
| | 12×8×2 | 3 L | 30×20×5 |
| | 13×9×2 | 3.5 L | 33×23×5 |
| Loaf Pan | 8×4×3 | 1.5 L | 20×10×7 |
| | 9×5×3 | 2 L | 23×13×7 |
| Round Layer Cake Pan | 8×1½ | 1.2 L | 20×4 |
| | 9×1½ | 1.5 L | 23×4 |
| Pie Plate | 8×1¼ | 750 mL | 20×3 |
| | 9×1¼ | 1 L | 23×3 |
| Baking Dish or Casserole | 1 quart | 1 L | — |
| | 1½ quart | 1.5 L | — |
| | 2 quart | 2 L | — |